1993

Pheasants

of the

Mind

A Hunter's Search for
a Mythic Bird

Datus C. Proper

Illustrations by Eldridge Hardie

Prentice Hall Press

New York   London   Toronto   Sydney   Tokyo   Singapore

⟨S⟩ P E C T A T O R

This book is meant to last
longer than the rest of me
so it is for Anna,
who puts denim flowers on my armor
and pastry hearts on the pheasant pie,
and pushes me to go hunting,
and pulls me back home.

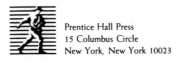

Prentice Hall Press
15 Columbus Circle
New York, New York 10023

Copyright © 1990 by Datus C. Proper
Illustrations © 1990 by Eldridge Hardie

PRENTICE HALL PRESS and colophons are registered
trademarks of Simon & Schuster, Inc.

Library of Congress Cataloging-in-Publication Data

Proper, Datus C.
    Pheasants of the mind / Datus C. Proper.
        p.   cm.
    Includes bibliographics references.
    ISBN 0-13-662750-1
    1. Pheasant shooting—United States.   I. Title.
  SK325.P5P76   1990
    799.2'48617-dc20   90-32999
CIP

Designed by Richard Oriolo

Manufactured in the United States of America

10 9 8 7 6 5 4 3 2 1

First Edition

Contents

Part III
Real Pheasants

Part IV
Dogs

PART V
Armor, Gun, and Flavor

Introduction

Hunting is not fiction, but it happens in the mind. It is the oldest and youngest thing in the world. It feels like dawn. Sometimes my teeth chatter while I am writing about it. It is irrational: The cock pheasant has a primitive cerebral cortex but enough wits to elude me. He runs me till I am too tired to think, stretches me till mind and body merge. Expect my organization to be driven by this bird-brained logic, mixing method and mood, how and why.

Parts I and II are about hunter as well as pheasant. Both are odd birds. It might have been less embarrassing to invent imaginary characters—especially when the villain was me—but I left the facts where I found them. The book is therefore nonfiction, according to twentieth-century rules; but nonfiction is a double negative. Do me the favor of pretending, instead, that this was written a couple of hundred years ago, before English speakers adopted *genres* and other unpronounceable notions. Pheasants remain stranger than fiction, too beautiful to be stuffed into a slot.

Beginning with Part III, there is more information on dogs, guns, gear, and methods. If you are young, start here, and then go look for a bird. This book aims to help you find it. Later you will have time to see where else the pheasant leads.

It leads back to sources: the accidents of time that make you and me behave as we do, whether we know it or not.

It leads into the future, because it thrives near the big towns where we increasingly live.

It leads us inside ourselves to a place we could not reach on purpose.

You can get there from here. The pheasant knows where it is going.

To the people in this book, my profound thanks. I am grateful also to the editors of *Field & Stream*, who encouraged me to chase pheasants in print before the book took shape. Here and there I have used paragraphs and passages (but no entire chapters) that appeared first in the magazine. They had things about old Trooper that I did not want to forget.

And thanks to the farmers in Montana, Pennsylvania, Maryland, Virginia, West Virginia, New York, New Hampshire, Nebraska, Colorado, and Ireland, who gave me days that I cannot repay.

DATUS C. PROPER
Bozeman, Montana
March, 1990

Part I

✦

Pheasants

of the

Mind

1

The Chase

Freedom's just another word
For something good to do.

ast fall the pheasants were spotty, meaning that they were in
some places but not in others; and a friend who had spent three
days hunting in the others commented, during our long drive home,
that he didn't mind because the ring-necked rooster was barely a
game bird anyhow. When pressed to list its defects, he said that it
was not a native, had no tradition, and was too gaudy to be a
gentleman. He did allow that pheasants might be all right in those
European driven shoots. The folks over there knew how to do things
right.

The hunter who made these comments was unaware, poor
fellow, that his driver (of truck, not birds) was a self-appointed
Defender of the Faith and Pheasants. Furthermore, I had worked in

Europe for eight years, during which time some nice people invited me to driven shoots. This calls for a policy statement. To anyone contemplating further such invitations: I am available. The Europeans deserve credit for making the most of their tight spaces. They make good lunches, too.

Meanwhile, on this continent there are still wide fields and wild pheasants, if that is what you like. It is what I like. I'd rather hunt one bird than shoot many. I want sunburned grass, golden stubble, gray barns, red rose-hips, dogwoods turning purple, and miles to go before I sleep.

Do not confuse wild with wilderness. It happens that pheasants thrive in some of our American wilderness, but we do not need them there. We need them near civilization, where they *must* be wild—unremittingly, ineradicably wild. Immigrants like the pheasant and brown trout refuse to go tame, even when we imprison them. They survive where native species cannot.

Back when dropping out was fashionable, there was a tune with this message:

> Freedom's just another word
> For nothing left to lose. [1]

That's a good idea gone wrong, a cheerless surrender. The pheasant shows the way. He is free in the interstices of humanity. He fights or dies, and cackles over the choice. He has only one song with one discordant line:

> Don't let the bastards wear you down.

Real freedom always has a *from* after it—freedom from noise and stench, perhaps, or from bosses, subordinates, cafeterias, bloodless triumphs, meetings, and chairs. Or from myself. Freedom and pheasants alliterate. They pry me loose, drag me through dust and thorns, resurrect me laughing.

I do not have to chase pheasants to catch freedom. I feel it when I ride my bicycle through old factory yards—watching Ailanthus trees pushing through cracks in pavement, paper cups blowing in the wind, sparrows quarreling. Even these places have a euphoric emptiness, but they are not beautiful. Farms are beautiful when their work is done and their colors change. Farms are where people grow our food and pheasants grow themselves.

I have chased pheasants from just above the Atlantic tidewater in Virginia to Colorado. They continue to the Pacific in California, and even dip south of the border into Mexico. Near the border in Canada they cross most of the continent again.[2] They live in at least thirty-nine states and six provinces. They are temperate birds like us Yankees, not boreal like the grouse family but still able to survive forty-below-zero nights in the brush behind my Montana home; not heat-loving like the quails but willing to put up with August in Texas.

These are the entrails of the country and pheasants lie near the heart. There are more people than pheasants but enough of the latter to make them one of the most abundant game birds in North America.[3] Everybody who sees them loves them, except for some cultivated hunters and more writers. We will ignore their problem till the third chapter. Meanwhile, talk to people in any small town from Franklin County, Pennsylvania, to the Willamette Valley of Oregon. Stop, for example, a few hours' drive east of my place, not far from the sign reading:

MINNOWS   ICE   DANCING

The sign is real but you'll have to excuse me for not revealing the place near it where I stop for a sandwich. Nothing ruins the tone of a neighborhood like a bunch of out-of-staters in red hats hanging around for hunting information.

A high-school coach there is drinking a beer. He remembers how roosters used to come in from the fields and run around shining on the green lawn behind his house. There were an awful lot of birds, back then. (But I don't want to know where there were a lot of them a long time ago. I want to know where there is one, right now.)

A farmer explains his solution for the decline in birds. He raises them in a pen, turns them loose to help the wild stock, and won't let anybody hunt. Not even his kids. (He is, as we will see later, loving the pheasant to death.)

A rancher brags about a three-legged blue-heeler dog who can still find a pheasant after those fancy pooches give up. (I wish that he would give my dogs a chance.)

A girl who drives to her job in the supermarket every morning mentions that she hears cocks crowing in a new field of wheatgrass. (We're getting closer.)

Her boyfriend tells how roosters used to flush from every patch of cover, and how free the country was before it blossomed with satellite dishes and NO TRESPASSING signs. Then he says "Heck, we're going out; come on along." He does not offer because the birds are plentiful. He invites me because a fellow ought to share what he can and pheasants are still free, sometimes.

He looks like good company and I'd like to accept his invitation. I'd like to get a pheasant, too. Instead I must hunt by myself and expect to get nothing. My two dogs are, for opposite reasons, equally unfit to be hunted with anybody else. The old one is in his thirteenth season and would die if pushed at a normal pace. I take him out mostly to hunt up memories. His successor is six months old and will be of no help for another year, if then. This season for him is just puppy-training. So I say thanks to the fellow who invited me.

The old dog makes me feel sorry for him. The young one makes me feel sorry for myself. Life is short and one bird season lost is one too many.

Old Trooper looks happy wobbling through the fields on skinny hips. He knows what to look for. He might find it if his nose were half as good as it used to be. Instead he potters around under bushes, sniffs the ground, finds where pheasants have been but not where they are. He is glad to follow me back to the truck. The stuff that is falling from a flat, gray sky is no longer drizzle and I am tempted to go home, but I know that I should first wake the pup from his little snooze and give him a learning experience.

Huckleberry does not need waking. I left him with a nineteen-by-forty-one-inch welcome mat (heretofore dogproof) as a cushion for his cage. The mat had twenty-five tufts of sisal per square inch. That amounts to 19,475 tufts, each with one hundred separate fibers. Huck has separated and redistributed 1,947,500 sisal fibers, neglecting no cranny of the truck. My wife's puppy has to be located by sound. He is asking where I have been and why I did not take him along. He's a cute lady's dog, all right. Cutest little shredder-mulcher you ever saw.

By the time he was four months old, Huckleberry had a way of looking deeply at his people, with eyes that understood more than they knew. "He's been here before," Anna would say—a very Irish comment previously reserved for human babies. I consoled myself with the thought that people are said to wind up looking like their dogs. If that is how it must be, I could find worse models.

You might suspect that such a pup, with such a lady, would become spoiled. You would be right. But there is another side to the story. This is also a lady who sits up at night with sick dogs, feeding them bits of chicken with her fingers. She did this for Trooper once when he decided to die in the prime of life. He ate to please her, and then he hunted four more years, spoiled, but not to death.

I expect the pampered Huckleberry to stay close to me, for protection against Harpies. (A Harpy, in case your mythology is rusty, is a kind of half-bird, half-woman with terrible talons, capable of flying off with pointer puppies. Cock pheasants fantasize about Harpies.) The pup, however, is as irrepressible as the hero he was named after. He busts a meadowlark, which is to say that he picks up its scent, then flushes it with no attempt to pause and point. He nearly catches the bird for the first thirty yards.

Huck's next conquest is a hen mallard on the creek. He smells her first, then sees her and flash-points: the briefest of pauses, but progress. He flushes the duck, splashes down in the middle of the stream, lunges to the other side, and chases her out of sight. This is how both pup and I discover that he can swim. It is the right attitude: Obstacles be damned.

It is the right dance, too. That the pup does not choose the right partners, at this age, means nothing, as long as he learns the music. The soul needs a dog who skims over the grass, looking good while he is looking around. Time enough later for the intensity of a full point. With it will come the eye-flash. He will not actually see the birds that he points—not often, at least—but his eyes will shine with the predator intensity that sheep dogs use to hold their charges. Perhaps pheasants feel such eyes too. I feel them.

A half-acre triangle of abandoned land surrounds a boggy spring. The patch is tall with grass, thick with weeds, and home to one cock pheasant, who plays a chord, or a discord. Perhaps this brief cackle is how a pheasant declares victory when rain turns back into mere mist. Huck does not know the sound yet. I reach into my shooting vest for a leash, with which I plan to lead him close to the bird and encourage sniffing around. "Here, pup," I will whisper, leading him back when he tries to dither off after muskrats. But first I have to catch him. He is dancing through the cover too fast, sure to bust the only pleasant of the day before I can get within shooting range. Then, thirty feet from the far edge, Huck points: head high, tail up, puppy foreleg cocked, baby-fat body tense. The real thing.

The advice I got was to let the pup run around for his first year, chase things, build up desire, do what he wants. What he wants, it seems, is to point a pheasant.

What I want is to shoot it. I have wanted to shoot many of them but never as much as I want this first one for a pup who is hunting a season too soon. There's going to be a flush, because the cock is pinned between us and a clear field. No. Never count on a pheasant. This one may be so wet that he does not want to fly, or he may have been sent to try us. Anyhow, he runs out into the open. He is eleven feet long and iridescent against drab grass. Huck is too low in the weeds to see what is happening, and I hesitate. Better wait for the bird to get in cover again or it will flush wild, before my pup gets close enough to point it. Huck loses the body scent and turns his head toward me, brow wrinkled quizzically. Did I do something wrong, boss?

You did it just right, buddy. (Tell me now: Do I know how to pick bird dogs or what?)

I see where the rooster enters a woodlot but Huck is not waiting for advice. He waltzes into the trees at the right place, which must mean that he is on scent. I'm dancing as fast as I can. Important to stay close: This new place is all trees and no ground cover, so the bird will not hold long.

Huck, thank goodness, is pointing again when I find him. We have fetched up against the rain-swollen creek, so this time the cock must surely flush, and it does, right across the water. It has grown to a length of sixteen feet. It is half hidden by limbs, but I have to try a shot. The bird falls on the far side of the stream. Huck crosses a second later, running on water. I hike up my shell-vest and follow, keeping my powder dry but not the wallet in my hip pocket. Huck points where the bird landed. It is no longer there. Then, instead of getting his nose down and trailing, my wife's idiotic pup jitterbugs away with his head high. I reckon he's after meadowlarks again but try to keep up. (Next year I will make my first million by selling a slimming pill, illustrating the advertisements with pictures of a hunter before and after the chasing season.)

In about three-hundred yards Huck is pointing at a national monument: our country's largest contiguous mass of thorns. His forehead is wrinkled again and it occurs to me that he does not know about retrieving much except slippers. I peel off the vest, leave the gun, flop belly-down in a puddle and start crawling under the bushes. It is not an obvious way to pursue happiness, but I must do right by both pup and bird.

Huckleberry crawls in to keep me company. Spoiled dog. Then he wriggles further under the thorns and emerges with two deep red scratches down his back. There is also a dead cock pheasant in his mouth. It is not as long as it looked flying—maybe just seven feet—but that's enough to hide much of a six-month-old pointer pup. Huck prances around on tiptoes with head in the air, just as he does when running off to bury Anna's best shoes. He doesn't retrieve, exactly, but he runs around me in diminishing spirals till there's nothing left to do but give me the bird. He watches me smooth its feathers and celebrate. His eyes have that curious look my wife noticed.

Then he licks the first blood off his back.

By comparison to other birds, the pheasant provides more of two emotions: chase and point. If you have watched a pup learning the game, I do not have to tell you what it is like, and if you have not, I probably can't. It feels like static electricity. There was another song about a girl getting "true emotion" from a television screen. I don't know the title—maybe Poverty In America.

The real thing is not supposed to be easy. Even if pheasants were not beautiful and not good to eat, I would still love them for pushing dog and me to our limits. A pointer needs what F. Scott Fitzgerald saw as America's special quality: "a willingness of the heart." Other birds hold as close, flush as wild, run almost as far, live in cover almost as difficult. No other does it all so often.

America will soon enough be tame. Pheasants and pointers and I will have blown away in the tons of topsoil that Montana loses to produce every bushel of grain. The land will have been divided into lots with white fences. Any game birds will be pen-raised and driven over guns, not hunted. There will be no choice. Our raw young sport will, by then, smell like a musty book. Some heir to my emotions will read this page and wish that he could trade a surfeit of order for a day of disorder.

Meanwhile it ought to be protean, not polite; seismic, not settled; a chase, not a chair. There should be confusion, sweat, gulps of cold water, buttons torn off, legs scratched, dogs red-striped. An intrepid pointer and I are two immigrants chasing an immigrant bird over a half-finished landscape, in on the end of a frontier, the beginning of a myth.

2

✦

Struggle
and Chance

Why We Do It

You never know when you will catch what you are chasing, but in good country you have faith. You stop and swing your gun three times where bright, unmown hay pushes against a thicket of twisted limbs. You dare the pheasant to flush. He is in the geometry of leaf and trunk, hill and field; you see how his colors will shine in the sun. Enough of this will conjure him up. You keep going. You do not intend to do violence to yourself, but the harder you try, the better your odds. This knowledge draws you out.

At the edge of fatigue comes relief: your head floats free of your legs. It feels a little like the sensation you get from a portable radio playing music in both ears as you ride a bus to work—but better. (I tried the recorded music once and did not like it because it got between mind and world. Bad as the commuter's environment was, an impermeable membrane between it and me was worse.) The hunter's high brings a heightened perception of wind in the aspens, mud squishing around boots, places where a pheasant ought to be. At this point it becomes easy to understand how visions came to Indians seeking them. A person who does mostly mental work needs this feeling; craves fresh air in the confines of brain and body. Perhaps everyone needs it.

You can get a runner's high, too, so it may have something to do with the blood pumped from legs that are weakening to a brain growing more active—a passing of the baton from the tired part of you to the fresh. I don't know, but the effect has a name: euphoria.

Euphoria feels as good as it sounds. According to the American Heritage Dictionary, it means: "1. A feeling of great happiness or well-being; bliss. 2. *Psychiatry*. An exaggerated sense of well-being in pathological cases involving sympathetic delusions." I leave the pathology to the pathologists and the physiology to the physiologists. What I think I understand is the music that the brain plays without benefit of radio. It is quite real, and here is how it works.

Your brain is constantly thinking, out there in the fields. You can confirm that easily next time you take a walk. You may not realize, however, that you are thinking in a language—presumably English, for most readers of this book. You are in a language mode even when you do not think aloud. This is by no means my discovery. I did not even grasp it till I came to know my own language by learning others. In time I found myself thinking in a couple of them, recognizing the words because they did not come so naturally as those in English. Language, it seems, is a way of forming thoughts, not just expressing them.

Your language is timed by your breathing. (This is easy to feel if you talk aloud to yourself as you walk.) Your breaths, in turn, are timed by the needs of your legs and heart and emotions. Musicians play the rhythms of the chase as if they were pounded out by a horse's four hoofs—but you march to the same drummer, biped, after you get going. Your chair-bound muscles stretch. Your tempo becomes upbeat, as regular as the farmland where pheasants live:

andante for the most part, allegro when dog strikes scent, presto when he trails the bird. And by now you are thinking in meter. You cannot help it.

Hunting is the oldest song, I guess. It would be nice to know the mother language that our ancestors evolved on the African plains. This much I can report: English is right because it has feet—literally. Feet (sequences of stressed and unstressed syllables) are the units of meter. Modern English-language poets sometimes soar above their language's feet, just to be different, and when they do, readers walk away. Conventional Spanish and French poets do not use meter, and their poems do not move my boots. I dream in Portuguese, sometimes, but I hike in English.

By the time you hear the beat, the thing that caused it has become important. It *must* be important to have done this to you. Therefore you try very hard to shoot the bird when your chance comes. You try even if you were not eager when you started walking. If you have not had the experience, you may find this baffling, but I imagine the long-distance hunters nodding yes, yes.

Whether you miss your chance or make it, you fix the pheasant's place by its coordinates. You will need to call it back later at the edge of sleep. The spot will be precise, then: the intersection of struggle and chance.[1] Your energy carries you far enough to cross the pheasant's path at some random place. Your dog's search meets the bird's collusion with cover. Your gun swings to intercept the path of flight. Your brain sends your trigger-finger a signal at the millisecond when the curves cross. The trajectories in time and space all intersect. True sports have such junctions and so does life, if played as a participant sport. Watching does not count.

One day you get no chances for all your struggle. Or, worse yet, you fail chances that you should have seized. Another time you make them all. If you consistently get limits, however, consider making the rules more difficult for yourself. Field sports are not about targets and scores. Score-keeping is necessary in competitions between humans, unattractive in competitions with weaker adversaries. Consistent scores of many to zero do not smell of struggle and chance. They smell of greed.

We oscillate between excess and fastidiousness, these days. We do not kill chickens in the kitchen and save their blood, as old recipes instruct, or make a holiday of butchering our pigs, as the Portuguese still do. We insulate ourselves from natural human death, too. I do not know whether it is a coincidence that our television sets are Roman circuses, displays of gladiators killing each other for the pleasure of an audience. Then there is the violence on streets, drug-pushers slaughtering for the privilege of selling effort-free thrills to the self-indulgent. Either this is not civilization or Freud was wrong when he saw civilization as holding unconscious impulses in check.

My family escapes most of the nastiness. We have no television set, see few films, live far from big cities. It is a boycott and more. The fact is that I am squeamish. So is my son, who never had a chance to get used to television. My wife is made of sterner stuff; I can bribe her to trap mice, which would take over the place if I were in charge.

Shooting our food is not like that. Sometimes I do feel sorry for woodcocks, ducks, bobwhites, and deer, in that order, but I hunt them, with restrictions to placate myself. We all draw the line somewhere. In Virginia, a neighbor installed an electric bug-zapper behind his opulently landscaped house. All night the infernal machine drew pretty moths to its light and fried them with sparks and sizzles. On the other hand, he would not teach his son to shoot an air rifle. Few of us today would kill a panda; many (but not me) are happy to squash spiders. I have no problem shooting rattlesnakes that threaten my pup. I do not want to kill any primate, any relative of the dog, anything young with big eyes. Do not bother to tell me that this makes no sense. I know that. It is anthropomorphism: the Panda or Cuddle Factor. It explains, I suppose, why the debate between anti-hunters and hunters is a dialogue of the deaf, between those who see hunting as an atrocity and those who suspect that the rest of life is the atrocity.

I feel few pangs for the cock pheasant. He is a dragon. If this be sympathetic delusion, make the most of it.

When I slay the pheasant, I kill, first, the dragon in me, which is the ugly one appearing in most Western art. Western painters have known about that greedy creature for as long as it has been threatening to consume us. They have, however, been ignorant of nature's dragon, the one that lures rather than repels. You are not to think that all dragons are ugly. Watch those that appear in Chinatown parades. These are the lovely dragons of the swamps, the ones that a Chinese artist could see running around in a rice paddy: serpent's tail, eagle's wings,[2] hawk's beak and eyes, cruel spurs. I have watched the cock pheasant chase off a fox.

At night I slay my dragon by the edge of the twisted forest. My son tells me that he does it too, and from the way Huckleberry runs and yips in his sleep, I conclude that pointer pups are in on the game. My wife, on the other hand, reports that the dragons in her country have been rendered extinct by a knight in shining armor. Perhaps the meaning of dragons is sex-linked. I do not know about this, but you may have confidence that *my* dragons are the real thing.

I clutch this reality as an antidote to indifference. We think of hunting and fishing as escape, and they are. They are escape from a society of escapism: from pervasive complacency, from media pitched to the lowest common denominator, from trivialization of thought, from the politics of blandness, from gladiators, celebrities, entertainment, scandals, the life synthetic.[3] A hunter chasing pheasants feels everything except anomie.

Pheasants make the fields and roadsides glow with feathers; women make the town swirl with skirts and fresh-washed hair. It is (I guess) no coincidence that the goddess of the chase is female, or that wives wear T-shirts reading "This marriage has been interrupted for the hunting season." Diana's pheasants and Eros's women populate adjacent sections of the male landscape.

Once, clothed in old jeans before old jeans were fashionable, I rode a decrepit motorcycle from my home in Montana to college in New York. North Dakota was the best part because the sun was shining and girls were on the sidewalks. My form of transportation seemed as romantic to me as it must have looked forbidding to anyone in her right mind. The streets shone with possibilities. As dungeon holds fair maiden, so might Fargo hold The Girl. I would scarcely have known what to do with her even if, by some miracle, her mother had not whisked her away from the hoodlum with bugs squashed between his black leather helmet and Lindbergh goggles. Thinking that she might appear was enough to make North Dakota beautiful.

"A trip to Florence or to Athens is one thing for a young man who hopes to meet his Beatrice on the Ponte Santa Trinita or his Socrates in the Agora," says Allan Bloom, "and quite another for one who goes without such aching need. The latter is only a tourist, the former looking for completion."[4]

Diana the huntress is another kind of completion: perhaps the only kind besides Beatrice the woman and Socrates the thinker. Hunting aches as much as the other two needs. Diana is distinctly older than thinking and older even than Eros, properly speaking. (Do not confuse Eros with mere reproduction.)

You can hunt with a bow and arrow or fishing rod instead of a gun. Perhaps you can hunt with binoculars and camera. I like them, but I use them mostly at comfortable times. The people I see hunting with lenses are near roads, in wildlife refuges, after breakfast, and sometimes in groups. They are more tourist than hunter. It seems to take a gun to get one into the lonely, thorny places before winter dawns.

In Diana's company you are not a tourist. You are not trying to peer into a distant secret magnified eight times by a lens. You are a hunter/forager like all wild animals. You have accepted the risks and discomfort that go along with climbing through the looking glass, into the secret.

When you descend from Diana's world and get back into your car, you leave the secret but take some of its emotions with you. You are now as far from real things as a tourist, but you see them differently. Bent cornstalks and collapsing barns are no longer objects, pretty or ugly. They are possibilities, sparks of excitement, stars that shine in the fields as you drive by. You must check them out next time. Hunting has populated the countryside with needs and meanings. The farm has become the faerie. It hides a pheasant.

There is a future in this. We will increasingly value bird hunting, especially with pointing dogs. The conviction settled on me, oddly, when a friend and editor asked me to investigate trends in trout flies over the last thirty years.[5] What I discovered was that there had been a boom in dry flies, and in imitative dry flies at that—those representing specific natural insects. Fishing with such flies is effective. It takes science, art, magic. It is visual, rational, demanding. It is fun. It is like hunting with a pointer, though more cerebral, not so relentlessly honest.

Call the dog's point a miracle or spell; either is close enough. Or consider it a gamble for high stakes between predator and prey. At core, the point is a prolongation of the pause before pouncing. All canids and felids (or at least all I have seen) do it. Why? Why not just jump on the prey without wasting time?

The answer became clear when Jeff Koski loaned me a "recall pen" so big that I could walk inside. We stocked the pen with a dozen bobwhites. For each training session, I catch a couple and put them out in the grass for the pup to point. At the end of the session, the birds remaining in the pen call the loose ones back in through a one-way door.

The catching is not as easy as it sounds, even in a pen. I cannot just walk in and start grabbing. If I do, all of the birds run or fly around. They confuse me. I reach for everything and catch nothing. Instead, I must stop and study, isolate one bird in my mind, ready my hand, then grab accurately. The pause gives me the advantage of surprise: I know exactly what I am going to do and choose when to do it. The bird must react to my initiative.

In the wild, however, the bird can conceal itself, which means that it too may gain something by waiting rather than flushing. The predator may pass by without knowing what it is missing. Gallinaceous (chickenlike) birds around the world often choose to hide rather than fly, when the ground-cover is thick enough. They know that they are most vulnerable at the moment when they jump from the ground: fully exposed, but still moving slowly. Predators are skilled at exploiting this moment.

The point, then, is tension. The pointer's art is tension crystalized, frozen in time like an insect in amber. Dog must persuade bird that any other course of action carries more risks than sitting still. It is a game of nerves. The pheasant is superbly adapted to it.

- On the one hand, its reluctance to fly means that it is exposed to the dog for protracted periods. (A bird that flies takes itself out of the game either because it escapes or is killed.)

- On the other hand, the pheasant lays a longer trail than any other bird hunted by dogs, and at the end of the trail must still be persuaded to sit until the human gets in a position to shoot.

The game, then is easy to join, long of play, and difficult to win: sporting, in a word. And the key to winning is tension.

The emotion of the point makes the game worth playing even off-season: Huck and I do it for half an hour on most winter afternoons. As opportunties for shooting constrict, more people will try no-kill hunting with a pointer, just as they now do catch-and-release fishing with a fly rod. They will get everything except the shot. The point will provide enough emotion (and complication) to compensate, for awhile. I would like to tell you that hunting under no-kill rules can keep dog and man keen forever, but canine and human pups both need the consummation. Old dogs and men do not need the shot as often as they did when they were young, but they need it sometimes. And all human families need the pheasant dinner.

Whatever the rules, we will need more of them to keep struggle and chance in balance as the natural world shrinks. Will our hunting mean less when it is more constricted? No: not if it is real hunting. Rules are part of that. Rules assure us that we are doing the thing right. The hunters who painted in the cave of Lascaux had art, so I would guess that they also had rules. If you have thought of those people as savages halfway down from the tree, have a close look at their paintings. They were as good as art gets. They had Picasso's economy and at least as much emotion. Artists then were like us, except that they stayed with two natural subjects: game, mostly, and then women. (A liberated twenty-first-century person like you would be bored with that old stuff, of course.)

Those ancient hunters would have wanted to stalk the wild bull according to traditions and codes, even when he needed no protection. They would have had myths.

Perhaps all of this seems primitive and forbidding. Perhaps you got this book to give to someone who deserves a present. You do not hunt yourself but you have read a little bit, trying to understand inexplicable tastes. How can a hunter shoot and love? Given a bit of time and sensitivity, it is natural—as natural as Achilles killing Hector, John D. Rockefeller turning philanthropist, or any teenage boy becoming a husband. Love and death are no harder to believe now than ten-thousand years ago.

3

~

B i r d   a n d   M y t h

In the first rank I will place the Pheasant,
as being indeed a Byrd of singular beauty, excellent
in the pleasure of her flight. . . .
Gervase Markham, 1655[1]

The partridge is the most abundant game bird in Montana. It is the original partridge, *Perdix perdix*, Partridge partridge, most partridgey of birds, partridge since before there was an English language. Most Montanans do not know that the bird exists. Those who see it are likely to invent their own name. When you stop at a farm to ask for hunting permission, you have to try a series of partridge synonyms: Huns? Quail? Redbirds? Little chickens? "Oh, *them,*" says the farmer. "Hell, go ahead. But don't mess with my phezzens."

Everybody knows the pheasant: knows it, moreover, by the name Jason gave it when he found it on the banks of the River Phasis. He brought the Phasian Bird back to the West with the

21

Golden Fleece. This bird has, therefore, the oldest of game-bird myths. It is still a pheasant[2] after all the centuries, all the odysseys.

Myths are always human, however, and in the New World we like to make our own. The pheasant—our pheasant—has a myth and an anti-myth, both of which explain something about the bird, more about its people. Consider this chapter a people-watchers' field guide.

The bird of our myth is good to eat and watch. You hear admiration in the voice of the teller. This myth, perhaps, is like Jason's. And like the original version, ours is transmitted orally, in rural areas, by people who do their own thinking.

The competing myth, or anti-myth, is likely to be transmitted by urban people, certainly book-people, like my friend in the first chapter. The anti-myth has force because its people are in charge of culture. Here is a way for you (the people-watcher) to identify them: Ask how they like the pheasant's looks. They will tell you that the cock is rather flamboyant for a person of good taste. They read this somewhere. It has not been an original thought for a hundred years. You need some history to understand.

Chinks

Sportswriters have favored the ferocious (cutthroat trout), the cute (timberdoodles), and the exotic (Huns). For a time, writers called pheasants "Chinks." It was like calling Joe Louis "the Brown Bomber." Usually no offense was intended. The label made clear, nevertheless, that pheasant's ancestors, like the boxer's, had immigrated from the wrong part of the world. Most of our traditions started in Europe and developed on the East coast. There are still easterners who know Europe better than their own country. The pheasant landed in the West and became the South Dakota state bird. It's not the kind of thing that plays on Broadway.

Perhaps you are a native, but neither pheasant nor I can claim to be. My family, like most, counts its American ancestry from the first off the boat, not the last; so let us start with Datus Sedgwick in 1630. If a generation is counted at thirty years, I am a twelfth-generation American. Pheasant generations take only a year, so the ringnecks I hunt have been Yanks for more than a hundred generations. Conclusion: Pheasants do not have as much history in America as I do, but they are at least nine times more American, genetically.

The pheasant's worst offense is success, which is not the kind of thing widely deplored on this continent. He is more handsome than you or me and the graduate of a tougher school, but in other respects he belongs in our society. Like us, he is big, aggressive, and heedless. Unlike us, he did not actually make war on the natives, but he knew how to live where they could not.[3]

Mind you, the history is muddled. People all over released pheasants and wanted to believe that they had accomplished something. English pheasants survived on Governor's Island and Long Island, New York, for a few years after introduction in 1733. There was a hunting season in Pennsylvania in 1902, with a negligible kill. The seminal pheasant transplant seems to have been to Oregon, in 1881. The American Consul General in Shanghai, Judge Owen N. Denny, achieved immortality by shipping twenty-eight Chinese birds to his brother's farm in the Willamette Valley. Oregon hunters shot nearly half a million pheasants in 1892, the first open season.[4] It showed the reproductive potential, under good conditions, of a bird that can raise ten or more young each year.

Two Immigrants

H.L. Betten hunted during that first Oregon season. He described the real pheasant pointer as "in a class by himself," and he admired the birds. The new birds were, however, so abundant as to be "almost pestilent."[5] From Oregon, the pheasant boom (pun intended) spread eastward. It was welcomed by farm boys and city men, but the law of supply and demand governs value. Pheasants were meat, not myth. Nothing easy is mythic.

If you wonder whether this really matters, consider how the brown trout would have fared in America if it had been found unsuitable for myth—which is to say, for fly-fishing. The old-world trout arrived on these shores at almost exactly the same time as the pheasant. The people who hated the immigrant trout knew that they must fight it on mythic grounds. Samuel G. Camp wrote in 1907 that "you have been more or less forcibly informed that the brown trout is a coarse fish; . . . that he lacks sporting blood and rises reluctantly to the artificial fly; . . . that, in fact, as a sporting proposition the brown trout is not to be considered."[6]

The original sin of brown trout and pheasant was the same. They (unlike native fish and game) had been learning about civilization for centuries before arriving in this country. Both species flaunted their knowledge. The old-world trout would sip real insects while refusing the angler's flies. The old-world bird would stand in a field looking heroic, then disappear when the hunter got out of his car.

Like the pheasant, the trout was accused of being too difficult, too easy, too successful—and ugly. Brown trout won't rise for our flies. (Pheasants won't hold for our dogs.) Those new trout won't fight, sir. (Pheasants fly like blimps.) Damned German fish are cannibals. (Pheasants did away with the native birds.) No color to those foreign trout. (Too much of it in pheasants.)

The trout, however, landed in the East and was escorted West by a vanguard of books. It had a myth too abundant to be erased. It was a popular failure and a literary success. The pheasant was a popular hit and a literary flop. Still is.

The trout's myth can be roughly measured by a recent catalog offering 1,249 old fishing books. The largest number of these is about fly-fishing for brown trout and its peripherals, such as fly-tying and hackle-raising. (There are so many peripherals that it is impossible to be precise. Other species of trout are usually lumped together with the brown, but under the rules it has established.) Many of the trout books cost more than a hundred dollars—some much more. The same catalog lists 369 books on small game, and two of those are on the hunting of the ring-necked pheasant. They are priced at eight and fourteen dollars.

The late nineteenth century was the golden age of British trout fishing, and the books reflected that. They set the standard for America too—eastern America, that is. And when we learned British rules, the brown trout rose, perhaps more readily than any other species.

The British did not help us much with the pheasant. In the Celtic fringe and a few other lightly populated areas, the pheasant was and still is hunted (with pointers and spaniels), but the people who wrote books had run out of land for wild sport. By the late nineteenth century they had, of necessity, "reduced pheasant shooting to an absolutely artificial pursuit".[7] Nothing mythic about that. Lacking guidance, we tried to hunt the pheasant like a native bird. It was like trying to get the brown trout to take Parmacheene Belles. The fish would not rise for our flies and the pheasant would not hold for our pointers. As far as I know, there are still no books on hunting the pheasant with pointing dogs.[8]

The Walleye and
The Carp

Perhaps you still suspect that I exaggerate the importance of myth. Here, then, is another fishy fable. In America, and certainly near my family's old summer cabin in Minnesota, the tasty fish called a walleye is mythic. The carp, on the other hand, is a "trash fish." It roots in the muck like a pig, thereby clouding the walleye's water. Our attitude is summed up in this news clipping, the date of which I have lost:

> Chicago (AP)—The Chicago River, once so
> polluted that only carp and associated nasty
> sediments survived, is making a comeback.

Change the scene to an English canal lined by fishermen. They would consider the carp a prize, but it is scarce. They settle for its finger-length relatives, creatures too small to be called panfish even if they tasted better than associated nasty sediments, which they don't.

The English fish as we do for trout, but they are much more skilled at catching the carp family. Their gear is elaborate; difficulty makes the sport. The point is not in the eating but the catching. You can guess what happened, therefore, when the walleye (alias zander) was introduced into English water. There were alarums and excursions. The new fish converted inedible cyprinids into food, but no matter. The material of myth was diminished.

The difference is in circumstance, not people. In England, fishermen had worked out satisfying tackle, techniques, and rules for catching the carps. The walleye came along and did not fit. In America, the same *human* thing happened with different animals. The introduced pheasant came into sharp conflict with the myths of the bobwhite and ruffed grouse. There is more on the grouse's myth in chapter 5; more on the bobwhite's in chapter 10.

Dogs

Man buys not dog but beauty, dignity, and blue blood. Dogs get names like "Count Noble" (a famous setter). Perhaps we Americans admire such titles because we are not allowed to hold them for ourselves. We marry our daughters off to European princes or buy a dog with class. Upper Class. The dog is perfect by revealed wisdom. Then a mere bird makes a fool of the aristocrat. No problem: Man can ignore evidence that remains hidden in the grass. Suppose, however, that another dog goes out and succeeds. Perhaps it is of a different breed. Perhaps it is of no breed, and accompanied by a fellow in coveralls carrying a rusty J.C. Higgins pump-gun. Imagine the snickers he directs at Count Noble. Then imagine the judgment that Count Noble's attendant passes on the pheasant.

Count Noble may be a dim bulb, but he may also be a good bobwhite dog that has been trained not to follow running birds. Running is what pheasants do best. His miscellaneous competitor, being uninhibited, keeps after them. He is a hybrid of clichés: wily rooster, drooling aristocrat, and clever farm dog. I'd love to take a mythic pheasant mutt to a field trial of the Missouri Headwaters Gun Dog Club[9]—a yaller dog with one ear up, one ear down, a happy grin, and major talent. So far I have not seen him. If the home-grown genius exists, he's hard to find.

So is the pheasant. Look for yourself. Look close.

When your dog goes on point, you have a better chance of seeing a little brown woodcock than a yard-long bronze, green, white, and dark cock pheasant. Clearly the big bird is more wary. It is also a stealth bomber, built to elude detection with a large payload. Camouflage is not the simple thing our grandfathers thought: The cock's coat of many colors is also a nature jacket. His habitat is bronze grass, green leaves, bright shafts of light, and deep shadows. His colors are an elegant solution.

Looking at all of the American upland[10] birds without sentiment (a kind of apostasy), I reckon now that the cock pheasant is the most beautiful. He is a tromp-l'oeil masterpiece of a kind that even nature does not often produce. When next you hear someone sniff at the pheasant, ask him how he likes the native wood duck, which has much the same color scheme in a version even brighter.

It took years of fasting and meditation for me to see the pheasant as he is. The fasting took place on November Saturdays near Washington, D.C., when gunning seemed more important than lunch. The meditation came during the rest of the year, and perhaps you do it too. You look away from your work, into a cup. In its dark liquid appears a woodlot, red and copper. At the edge there is a rail fence half-smothered in green honeysuckle. Between you and the tangle there is thick, bleached grass. A dog points, one foot raised, muscles quivering under shiny hide. You take another step. A cock is suddenly in the air, heading for a gap in the woods. Your reflexes resolve the blur, separate it from background, slow the violence. Gun-barrels struggle toward intersection with chance. The world narrows to a bird the color of autumn.

Part II

Love and Death

4

✦

Nebraska

Let this be said about Halsey Davidson, bless his soul: He got out of his car to shoot pheasants. Then he walked far enough that he would not blow the chrome bust of Pontiac off the hood of his prewar sedan. It would have been easier to slide the gun out the window. This was in the good old days of 1945, when birds did not panic till they saw man detached from car. They were as innocent as pheasants come, back then.

We saw six cocks within range. One flew before we got organized. Another flushed from the thick roadside grass, which no one mowed or sprayed in those days, and Mr. Davidson missed three shots with his full-choked Winchester Model 97 pump gun (12-gauge, of course). He ground-strafed four birds, of which two flopped around and expired. Of the other two, one sprinted off across fallow fields, faster than speeding #4 Super-X shot, leaping tall clods at a single bound. I chased the next runner, reckoning that I could do no worse than Mr. Davidson and learning that I could do no better, either. Pheasants can outrun some dogs and all humans, even motivated eleven-year-olds.

Not every child would remember details of guns and loads, but I had the Winchester pages in the Stoeger's catalog memorized. Those were good guns. They were like 1930s cars, halfway between the primitive and the decadent. Early guns were handmade and modern guns are machine-made, but the old Winchesters were hand- and machine-made, cheaper than those made before and more inspiring than those made since. You could have affection for a gun like that and still afford to buy it. The company would not have flopped around and expired if it had been able to keep on making such guns forever.

The model I was saving for was the semi-hammerless single-barrel (12-gauge, of course), the only one that seven dollars would buy half of. Dad must have concluded, as my savings increased penny by penny, that someone had best show me what to do with a shotgun. The problem was that we had no car to get out of town. Guns and cars and nations all seem to reach a peak at about the same time and I think maybe it was 1945, but the Propers were a little behind the curve.

Mr. Davidson had a car. The hunting he showed me was not what I had expected, but it was better than Omaha.

One of our neighbors in Omaha had fried an egg on the sidewalk, just to prove something. The white cooked right away but the yolk (an old-fashioned, farm-raised, yellow yolk) still looked soft and flat, like one of my mother's soufflés, when a dog came along and ate the experiment. Mr. Davidson took me hunting not long after that. The reward for Midwestern suffering is a time when the world cools off and the part beyond town—corn and hay and sun—is all the color of yolks.

We found birds near Omaha because nobody else was hunting: The boys were not back from victory yet. There were no posted signs, no other hunters, and lots of pheasants. I wanted to get out and roll around like a dog on a good-smelling place. Mr. Davidson preferred to cruise in the Pontiac but agreed to walk through one very small cornfield, the way sportsmen did it in the magazines. No birds flushed and he said "you see?" But I didn't.

By mid-afternoon, the yolkiest time of the day, Mr. Davidson didn't want to strain his eyes looking for things sneaking around in the grass, either; he wanted to try my slingshot on big dairy bulls with those funny targets swinging down between their hocks. Must have hit one because I remember him saying "bull's-eye," though what he was shooting at was as far from the eye as you can get on a bull.

Mr. Davidson donated the brace of birds and Dad taught me how to pluck them. Then we removed the plumbing and there was an odor most foul. Pheasants smell higher than other game birds, with the possible exception of wild turkeys. The smell has nothing to do with spoilage but persuades most beginners to do everything wrong: scrub, sanitize, give the dressed birds away. We did. We gave them back to Mr. Davidson. I had to take the bus across town to get rid of the foul fowl. This was another aspect of the sport that no magazine had explained: The day after the shooting was the more active, a sort of reverse scavenger-hunt. I suspect that the spoils of our ground-strafing raid wound up in a garbage can.

As good old days go, those seem so recent that the yolk is still runny. Nebraska was a place to break the shell, a place where soufflés and hunters had no occasion to rise. My Nebraska had no real pheasants. It had no bird dogs, walking, pesticides, crowds, progress, angry farmers, rules, compunctions, fees, money, defeat, hunger, good food, tradition, or myth. All it had was my first time. It was half-baked.

As good old days go, those were would-have-been-good days. What I needed was to import a little knowledge from the 1990s. It would be nice to think that this book will help some skinny Nebraska kid to figure it out.

5

New Hampshire

Many writers insist that this royal bird
[the ruffed grouse] is a very
unsatisfactory one to pursue for sport, and
they have written columns in its
vilification and are unsparing in epithets,
condemning some of its characteristic
habits. All of which goes to prove
conclusively that the same writers have
scant knowledge of the subject. . . .
S.T. Hammond, 1898[1]

Mr. Mitchell seemed shrunk by the wash of years. His double-barreled Parker shotgun was almost as tall as he was. He wore boots laced to the top of skinny calves, knee-breeches that tucked into the boots, a battered gray felt hat, a flannel shirt, and a hunting vest from the 1920s. There was a mismatch of costume and period, intent and capability. His gun's barrels were worn shiny and his clothing had been used hard, once upon a time, but now he was slow even to climb in the car. I was very young but not entirely lacking in reverence. If Laurence Mitchell had been a figure in stained glass with the sun shining through him, he would have been my favorite church window. When he appeared instead for a hunting trip, my reaction was different, and I confess it to launder my shame.

I thought: He's going to slow me down. Can't let him out of sight because he is going to die.

This all happened in 1948 so the skeins of it are tangled, but they have not faded. Mr. Mitchell was New Hampshire and New Hampshire was the oldest place in the world. I have visited the original Hampshire since and watched the sun shine into the Winchester cathedral through Izaak Walton. Everything is neat and polished in those parts. There is little of the ache that one feels where nature has overrun the works of man. If you want to get fussy, Mr. Walton was born before Mr. Mitchell, but memory is not organized like that. My New England is more decayed than the country it was named after.

The mold is a noble rot. It rises from the pages of books written by dead men. It rises from crumbling cellar holes where women once stored provisions, from apples falling where no children pick them up, from red leaves drifting over illegible headstones, and from a wee old man wobbling after grouse that he can no longer catch.

· Larry Mitchell looked as if he had been evolving in New Hampshire since the ice age, but in fact he had grown up in New Mexico. I don't know when he was born. He once rode shotgun on a stagecoach, which would have made him older than the average high-school freshman. He worked his way to New England on cattleboats in 1900. I got to the same place in 1947: a prep school back East that gave scholarships to boys out West. Back East and out West were points on my compass. I may have been the only student that year to arrive at the Exeter drugstore-and-bus-depot by Greyhound, but it looked familiar to me. If I had reconstructed my ancestors (as some scholars today try to reconstruct the proto-Indo-European language), the genesis would have smelled like New Hampshire in autumn, close and far and new and old.

Mr. Mitchell is the hero of this chapter, but he is hollow. I mean, he was a real person but I did not take time to know the man between skinny old frame and fossil clothes. He was essences without flesh: a smell of Hoppe's Number 9 gun-cleaning solvent and a pair of sharp blue eyes. He could bend over suddenly in the Old Schoolhouse covert and pick up an Algonquin arrowhead that other eyes had missed for three-hundred years. I could not then, and still cannot, understand his power to shift instantly between the hunter's focus (a mid-range sweep) and the ground at his feet. I should have asked questions. I was too eager to chase something: the grouse upstream of school, where a bridge crossed from the playing fields into the woods, or the cock pheasant downstream where the Squamscott was still tidal. Maybe little Larry Mitchell felt the same way in 1900.

By 1947, Mr. Mitchell was a retired prep-school teacher and a hunter, mainly, of memories. In between us, playing liaison, was an active-duty hunter named Mr. Bill Bates who was old enough to know about birds and young enough to show me. He was an active-duty teacher, too; and a teacher is an advanced form of professor—the kind that knows not only his subject but his pupils. Bill Bates taught English in the mornings, then grouse, woodcock, pheasants, and black ducks between afternoon classes. Enough feathers drifted down to add their musty smell to my mindscape. In the first years Bill Bates pulled the trigger but I flushed birds out of the thick stuff, yelled "mark right!", retrieved (not as well as most dogs), and plucked the feathers (better than most dogs). Then his wife cooked the birds. Mrs. Betty Bates could roast them in sherry sauce till they tasted as good as cookies from home. Not many people know how to do that.

The other revelation was Bill Bates's library. Picture a New England saltbox house with lady's-slipper orchids in the garden and eight rooms inside, four to a floor. Everything was old and square, with ceilings upstairs that were four inches lower than the top of my head. A ground-floor room had a wall lined with books. Their covers were little doors. I opened them and walked back through the years, out into the woods.

The best of the time-and-space trips was in a book by William Harnden Foster.[2] He is yet another hero of this chapter. New England was like that: none too wealthy in wildlife or money but bulging with heroes. Foster had grown up just across the Massachusetts line. He had hunted some of the same New Hampshire coverts[3] that Bill Bates showed me, near Epping. Foster had published his book in 1942—just forty-four years after the S.T. Hammond book that furnished the quotation at the head of this chapter. In those few years, attitudes had swung 180 degrees. No one disdained the ruffed grouse now. On the contrary, it had acquired the most powerful myth of any game bird, surpassing even that of the bobwhite or the old-country red grouse, both of which had a head start. The latter birds were and are excellent game, with one vulnerability: They could be shot with little effort if one had enough money. They were gentlemen's game.

A "gentleman's" anything is a sales job. Gentlemen's guns are expensive ones that do not show much wear on their casehardening. A gentleman's sport is one in which others are paid to do the walking. Foster was obviously a gentleman—he even wrote of grouse "shooting" as if he were British—but what he did early in this century was real, sweaty, pants-ripping pa'tridge hunting, in the company of New England gentlemen with callused hands. And then he ended formation of the grouse myth with its telling. Like art, myths are original. If what you are doing is fashionable, you are too late.

Foster was the grouse's Homer, catching the myth rather than building it from scratch. Much of that had been done by Burton Spiller, in another good book[4] and in articles for *Field & Stream*. Spiller was a better writer than Foster and just as knowledgeable. But Foster produced the most beautiful hunting book ever.

The secret, I think, was in the dignity of small things. Foster was a trained artist who knew the New England of abandoned farms. He knew its people, birds, dogs, and guns. He put them all in his drawings. Then he provided a written counterpoint, prose to explain magic. Nothing in his sport was too small to deserve reverent attention. The picture of his first grouse shows a subtle curve of the wings that few people would recognize: it means "bird that will land dead." The shotguns he drew can be identified by their lines and engraving: Parker, Purdey, Woodward. Opening the book is like opening the gun. You hear the hammers cock, smell the powder, laugh at the bolting dog, cheer the escaping grouse.

Bear in mind that this was a time when representational painting had become passé,[5] when "manuals" and "literature" were supposed to be different kinds of communication. Foster ignored fashion and thereby created one. He did for the grouse what Frederic M. Halford's books did for dry-fly fishing: wrote the rules. The difference is that anglers like to rebel from Halford, while grouse-hunters become enchanted by Foster as soon as they aspire to anything beyond slaughter. I defy you to see his book without wanting to go grouse hunting, and to do it, moreover, as Foster did it. His book became the grouse-hunter's Koran, the model of perfection, language of paradise. Try to understand the passions of New Englanders. They may answer long questions with "ayup," but more is going on in their heads.

There is in sports a great deal of loose writing about saints, rituals, icons, and holy places. I am trying to be more careful. For a parallel to Foster, look to Albrecht Dürer's famous hare.[6] It is respectable to see reverence in images at least five-hundred years old.

Myths are always about people being tested, and the New England ruffed grouse is a stiff test. We covered the miles, Bill Bates and I, and sometimes Mr. Mitchell. With him, however, we covered a lot of them in Mr. Bates's 1941 convertible, pretending that we were going to hunt. The car was one of us. Its blue paint had faded to eye-color; its engine grumbled like an old bird dog that wants to be told to get going so that it has grounds for complaint. This, however, was in the days before Henry Ford's cars had become appliances. The chassis might emit arthritic creaks but it did its duty. We crept down the gravel road in the Oaklands or followed back lanes to other coverts: the Big Blackberry Swale, the Crab Tree Cellar Hole, or the Mae West, named for a big beech tree with two uplifting burls. These are real names but you won't find them on the map. They are real-hunter names, not real-estate names.

I did not see many birds but I heard much about them. Teachers of English talk, even in New England. Mr. Bates and Mr. Mitchell sat in the front seat and I sat in the back, listening. It dawned on me that this is what men do. They do not get together just for company. They join for great enterprises like making war or building railroads or hunting birds. To solve the problems, they talk. In this they achieve a limited, undemanding closeness. They do not talk about that. They talk about weapons and transportation and the way things used to be done, back when they were done right. But for the old boys, the talk becomes more important than its subject.

For me, it was easier to relax and enjoy the conversation if I had first been turned loose to crash around in the woods and meadows, missing grouse and chasing pheasants. An hour or two of that brings on a philosophical disposition. Or maybe the talking just becomes a way to avoid physical exertion.

By my senior year I had my own 12-gauge Winchester. It was a double-barreled Model 24, bought second-hand for sixty-five dollars with some of my summer wages. The Academy, bless it, let me take hunting as a fall sport, under the supervision of Bill Bates. Some days he took me and Mr. Mitchell. Other afternoons I peddled off to the woods on my bicycle, shotgun tied to the handlebars. In principle, I knew how to hit flying objects, having studied Mr. Foster's diagram. The principle worked—on ducks. The upland birds were so tricky in the air that they tempted me to shoot them sitting. Can't say for sure whether temptation ever won out. Some memories should be allowed to acquire a patina.

This much I can report with precision: the grouse were careless when picking grit from back roads, and New Hampshire had abundant stone walls behind which a boy could sneak. The grouse would also flush, most of the time, when I walked near them in the woods like a real hunter. Each flush offered an opportunity to waste two expensive shells. Replacements would come from a box of loose ammunition on the counter of a sporting-goods store run by another ancient man. Meanwhile, being out there in the woods, all dressed up with no shells to shoot, was one of life's major frustrations. I felt it so often that I am still hoarding shotshells. They make me feel prosperous.

The pheasants were less abundant than grouse but not as good at weaving through the trees. They were thus easier to hit, theoretically. The problem was that they would not flush in range. They would run off and rise at a safe distance, sending me a flash of color and a cackle. They also refused to pick grit while I sneaked up on them. I could hunt grouse without a dog but the pheasants seemed hopeless.

Eventually I killed a bird flying. (Ducks, you understand, do not count as birds for upland gunners.) It was down by the Squamscott River on the opening day of pheasant season. The resident cock flew right down the grade toward me, as in Mr. Foster's diagram. Raise gun carefully. No, the pheasant was a hen, and therefore illegal. Lower gun dejectedly. The hen was flying slower than usual. Then it passed me and I saw that it was a grouse. Raise gun abruptly. There was no time for calculation, barely time to swing barrels through target. The grouse came down, centered in the pattern of shot. It was the only graduation day that I still recall in detail.

There is a part of if that I am again ashamed to mention. I was thrilled with my grouse but wished, just a little, that it had been the cock pheasant, twice as big and in Technicolor. Then I thought of Mr. Foster and tried to rectify my attitude.

Mr. Bates was delighted when he shot one of New Hampshire's rare pheasants. Mr. Mitchell, I think, saw them as a lesser breed without the law. Like most New Englanders, he had persuaded himself that the pa'tridge was a superior bird even on the table. If I had asked Larry Mitchell whether the pheasant measured up as a game bird, he would have said "not on your teetotum!"—his way of dealing with impertinent propositions.

Mr. Foster was too good an artist to call pheasants ugly, but he did not like what they did to hunters. Pheasants had been plentiful and conspicuous for a time after they reached New England. When the Massachusetts season for them opened in 1914, Foster saw "a stampede to the local town clerk's offices for hunting licenses, and another to borrow some sort of shotgun. Automobile loads of tyros drove the country roads and, from their seats, ground-strafed pheasants in farmers' fields, gardens, and even front yards. Others ganged up and, walking abreast, beat meadows and swales, firing veritable salvos at every pheasant that got up ahead. Fortunately there were others whom the pheasant attracted who set out to be real sportsmen. They bought dogs, hunted where they would not be an affront to common decency, and tried to uphold the code. . . . In the meantime practically every farmer and rural landowner in the pheasant areas had been forced to post their land. . . ."[7]

For Foster and Mitchell, on the East Coast in the early twentieth century, pheasants were interlopers. Nationwide, however, pheasants and ruffed grouse got started as sporting species at about the same time. The first American book on upland game does not even mention the ruffed grouse.[8] Hunting for it with dogs and guns did not start seriously till the 1880s—at most a decade before the first pheasant season opened in Oregon. By the turn of the century (as Hammond's book makes clear) the grouse was still held in much lower esteem than the woodcock. Even today, hunters in the West look on pheasants as the best of birds and grouse as tree-sitters waiting to be potted.

For me, New England's grouse and pheasants played in the same orchestra. What I heard was not dissonance. They stood on mossy logs not far apart. The grouse drummed with his wings in the woodlot. The pheasant stood on his toes at the wood's edge, tipped his head up, and blew a brassy cackle. By the time Bill Bates and Larry Mitchell showed me around, it did not matter much whether the bird that flushed was dressed in shadows or a suit of lights. The only newcomer was me, and I felt at home.

Not long after I left, Mr. Bates took Mr. Mitchell hunting when the leaves were in color. New Hampshire's orbit swings very close to heaven at that time of the year. The old man picked up his gun, walked into a grouse covert by himself, sat on a granite boulder, and then lay back to rest a little. He did not wake up. I used to think that he was out of style, but I've rectified my attitude. Larry Mitchell knew how to do everything right.

6

> ✦

Pennsylvania

In 1969, the pheasant boom was near a peak and my car was near a meltdown. The pheasants were in the limestone country of Pennsylvania, just ninety miles up the road; the car was a 1951 Oldsmobile, behind my apartment in Washington, D.C. It held me back like a jealous spouse, Hydra-headed transmission sprouting two new troubles for every one amputated, dashboard polymers heat-shrinking into a scowl.

Dick McCormack pried me loose from the clutching plastic: found transportation, persuaded me that I did not have to work every Saturday, even scouted the pheasants. Dick worked for a political party with intermittent demands. He had spent summer weekends in the fields and knew where the birds were, not by county but by acre. Of course I said that I would go with him on opening day. Bruce had a nice new car so Dick drafted him, and Bruce brought along Linda, and Linda changed the whole complexion of the weekend. For one thing, we did not have to stop for coffee. Linda had a laugh that would have made a blind man wake up and propose. None of us were blind. She was tall, brown-haired, and slim where women are supposed to be slim, but not elsewhere.

Bruce was in the Foreign Service, like me, but he looked like a recruiting poster. He gave me one of those odd *déjà vu* feelings till I remembered the association: He was the elegant cavalry officer in an old print, explaining the role of horsemen in 1914. "We keep war from becoming a mere vulgar brawl," the caption had said. Linda believed it.

Dick knew of two good cornfields, so we split the group, Bruce and Linda loping off together. This was the time when women had just started wearing blue jeans and some critics thought they looked bad. None of the critics had watched Linda climbing barbed-wire fences. Dick and I moved off with concentration gradually returning and reflexes honed extra-sharp.

The legal shooting time was still a few minutes off, so we stood at the end of our strip of corn, staking a claim to it. My stomach was queasy. Always is for the first day. There is the problem of avoiding other hunters, some of whom go out only once each year. There is the fear that some of the tyros will be using big #4 shot and won't mind where they aim it. There is the fear of not finding a pheasant and the fear of finding one. Most of all, I suppose, there is the fear of missing an easy shot and going home birdless.

The shooting started too early and swelled, in the distance, to something approaching a Civil War skirmish. Lots of people were getting pheasants and we weren't. Dick and I turned off the rest of the world and started to walk through the corn, twenty-five yards apart, each of us near an edge.

The first bird up was a hen taking an awful chance, flying between two gunners twitching and lusting. But we walked on. Fifty yards farther there was a clatter of wings in the tall stalks ahead of me. The head that lifted out of the corn this time was green with a white ring. I shot. The cock collapsed as it cleared the stalks. I sprinted and there it was, flopping. Done. I stood a moment in remorse, watching the fallen warrior. Like hell I did. I grabbed Thanksgiving dinner by the neck and waved it at Dick and made grunts of lust's labor won. To describe the event as incredible is indeed not credible, considering that I had done what I fully intended to do, but the first pheasant of the season stimulates, among other things, cognitive dissonance.

Dick attested the triumph by a broad grin and a fist waved over his head. Good man, Dick. Then we walked a hundred more yards and I repeated my feat, except that the victim this time was Christmas dinner. Dick offered another broad smile, though perhaps not quite as broad as the first. Pheasants have a way of giving the same hunter all the shots, all day. This day was fifteen minutes gone and I had my limit. We laid my two cock pheasants out in the car and I gloated. Dick seconded the gloat. Then we gulped lukewarm coffee and watched for Bruce and Linda through a windshield increasingly pocked by drizzle.

I said nothing about the weather. A hunter with a limit must mind his manners. I could not hint that hunting in glop is no fun, because if Dick wanted to do it I would have to go along, gleefully. A single, dogless hunter has a hard time surrounding birds. Of course Dick wanted to go and of course the glamorous couple did not show up to suggest a dry lunch at a restaurant where Linda could slip into something more comfortable.

Dick's subconscious may have been active too, because he led the way to a perfectly rounded, feminine hill—a miniature mountain that, if some Frenchman had found it, would surely have been called Grand Teton before the name could be misapplied to a crag in Wyoming. We walked around and around, spiraling slowly up the hill. I stayed thirty yards below so that Dick would reach every bird first. Even so, three or four cocks presented chances that I could have taken if I had not already shot my limit. There was a lot of game in those days.

Dick flushed seven legal pheasants and missed two shots at each of them. He was no worse with a shotgun than me: Both of us had learned by snap-shooting at grouse in the woods, and we weren't very good at that either. A snap-shot is one that you throw ahead of the bird, aiming at the place where you think it will be when your shot arrive—several hundred little pellets in a group. You don't swing your gun. You guess right, sometimes, when you have fast young reflexes and slow targets: grouse that have just flushed or pheasants rising nearly straight up out of corn. Birds flushing low, far, and fast are a different proposition. The intersection of shot and target is impossible to calculate, then, unless you swing your gun at the bird's speed or faster. It is art, not science. You paint the bird out of the sky with a moving brush, forgetting geometry.

Neither of us knew how to do it. And so we waltzed on up the hill through wet, knee-high grass.

> VERSE: Slosh, slosh, slosh, slosh, slosh, slosh.
> CHORUS: Bang-bang! Damn!
> Repeat.

It was perfect pheasant cover, perhaps the kind of tall, protective grass in which the birds had evolved, back by the slow River Phasis. The only thing that seems remarkable is that so many chose to flush. Today they would run off and hide. One tried it even then—Pennsylvania's senior pheasant, the rare bird that lives for several seasons, a cock over three pounds with wicked spurs and two-foot tail. He ran to the very top of the hill (whatever the French would call that) and exposed himself only because Dick knew enough to palpate the last bit of cover. The bird launched and flew downhill with no waste motion, gaining speed from strong wings and gravity. Dick aimed his gun carefully, like a rifle, which is the surest of all ways to bring on that old refrain: "Bang-bang! Damn!"

Then, much to his credit, Dick laughed and shook his fist at the cackling foe and yelled, "I'll get you next week!"

We did not quit. No sir, we were not quitters, or at least Dick was not. We went to the place where the birds seemed to have flown, but they hadn't; and then we walked to more places. Each of us shot a couple of bobwhites, which cheered Dick a little. Rabbits came out to cavort in the drizzle. I did not shoot any because my wet canvas jacket already weighed twenty pounds or so, and a large, soggy rabbit did not seem like a congenial addition. Dick shot. It turned out that he had no game-pocket, so he stuffed each victim in mine. He did not stop till he had seven rabbits, or rather till I had seven of his rabbits. By then, feet and heads and floppy ears protruded from every orifice of my Duxbak. Most of the weight was in the back of the coat so that part hung low. The front rose till its top button lodged against my throat. While staggering to the car with seven sopping cottontails swinging from my Adam's apple, I formulated a new policy on game-carrying but thought best not to announce it till Dick had a pheasant.

Bruce and Linda still had not returned. We speculated that they had found something better than rabbits—perhaps a cozy barn, with hayloft. The drizzle stopped so we went to one last covert, a woodlot by the road. I left my jacket with the game-pocket behind in an effort to implement the new policy gradually.

We found where the pheasants had gone, but they kept flushing well ahead of us because the second-growth trees lacked ground cover. At the end, a recent cutting had let in sun and encouraged honeysuckle, briars, even poison ivy. Something had to be there, and it was. I beat the covert and flushed the pheasant back over Dick.

Strange bird, this one: It lifted out of the ivy and danced through the tree tops slowly, almost teasing. Perhaps because of the surfeit of rabbits, I wanted to shout "let it go," but that would have been silly. My friend deserved the real thing and got it. The bird died in a way that I have never seen in another, before or since: kept its wings outstretched and swirled slowly down like a child's glider. The descent was so slow that the pheasant settled gently, wings still spread, head limp, drop of blood on the beak.

There was another odd thing. Pheasants vary in color, but we had never seen one as beautiful as this. It was young, smaller than usual, but glowing in every detail. I have since read that female pheasants occasionally put on the cock's plumage in a form still prettier.[1] Dick and I did not know that, but we did kneel to look this time, both of us. Then a breeze ruffled the feathers and Dick picked the bird up gently.

Bruce and Linda were back at the car, thoroughly wet, so they had hunted seriously. They had only a couple of rabbits and a bobwhite. Linda did not mind, but then she was just along for company, with no gun. Bruce was silent. On the way back, she curled up against him to keep warm and he did not put an arm around her. I would have traded the Thanksgiving and Christmas dinners for a chuckle from her, and Dick, no doubt, would have swapped even his most beautiful of pheasants, not to mention seven sopping rabbits.

Dick and I kept it up, hunting every Saturday when I could get away, plus Veterans Day and Thanksgiving. My Oldsmobile carried us without fuss, a shrew tamed. At the end of the season, I asked Dick if he had been in touch with Washington's most handsome couple. He was surprised that I had not heard. Bruce had invited Linda to some fancy ball, then showed up on the evening of it, when she was already dressed for the occasion, and told her that he was taking someone else instead. Her parents found her dead the next morning, still in her gown.

Dick then learned that Bruce had pushed another young woman to suicide at an overseas post. I groped for the right words. "He's a swine," Dick said. Those were the right words.

The opera was not over. Bruce was found, not much later, to have terminal cancer. I do not know when the disease started, or why, or if he accepted it. The opera is over now. I have changed the lovers' names but not their story. Dick will vouch for it. His name is real and mine is too (strange as it looks on a book cover).

Dick and I tried to go back for the trophy pheasant on the hill of soft grass, but some nonhunter from the city had bought it and put up no trespassing signs.

Part III

Real Pheasants

7

><

What Happened?

There are still those who shy at this prospect of a man-made game crop as artificial and therefore repugnant. This attitude shows good taste but poor insight. Every head of wild life still alive in this country is already artificialized, in that its existence is conditioned by economic forces. Game management merely proposes that their impact shall not remain wholly fortuitous. The hope of the future lies not in curbing the influence of human occupancy—it is already too late for that—but in creating a better understanding of the extent of that influence and a new ethic for its governance.

Aldo Leopold[1]

"**D**iplomacy," someone said a long time ago, "is easy on the head and hard on the feet." So is pheasant hunting if you do it wrong. I am a foot expert, as some of my friends and all of my enemies will tell you, but I did think that I knew where to find pheasants in Pennsylvania. There was a circuit of coverts that were life-blood to me and my old German shorthaired pointer. On opening day in 1982, Trooper and I hunted them from the minute we could legally do so until sundown.

We hunted the woodlot of the beautiful pheasant and found a house where the holding cover used to be. We hunted up the spring run, over the beaver dam, through the osage oranges, then back over

51

the run and down the other side. All we saw in there was a deer, and four more hunters. We hunted the brushy orchard by the covered bridge, where we saw an English pointer dragging a long chain, and then two fellows trying to find him. We hunted the two hidden woodlots down behind the school. We drove by other coverts that had cars parked beside them and lines of red-hatted men moving through. On this loop I would have expected to find thirty birds in the 1960s and perhaps half that many in the 1970s. In 1982, on the first Saturday of November, we found a grand total of one hen. Not a single cock for Thanksgiving dinner.

Trooper had to be lifted back into the rear of the station wagon, groaning softly, and I think his complaint had something to do with the lousy intelligence behind this operation. I sagged on the tailgate and peeled old boots from new blisters and tried to explain that, shucks, we had been overseas quite a while, and how was I supposed to know that the good old days were over?

We drove home with at least one of us wondering why fall had bothered to come around at all. Without birds, there was no sense in the frost ripening the persimmons or the wind rustling the cornhusks or the trees turning the color of pheasant feathers. There was no point in watching the roadsides as we drove along, because there was no life in the tangles of greenbriers and roses. Why bother to pick wild apples and puffball mushrooms when there was no pheasant sauce to go with them?

The old coverts were more than just good places: they were dreams in color, faded now like my father's 16-millimeter movie films. Dick McCormack had warned me. He had hunted one whole season without getting a bird. He knew a lot about pheasants, too; knew how to work every cover to the end and throw a rock in the last clump of it. But Dick did not have a dog.

By 1982, Trooper had seven years of hunting experience, the first three in America and four more in Europe. Before that, at the age of eleven months, he had gone into a field trial open to all breeds. He won the puppy class, then the derby, then the gun-dog, and then the dog-of-the-year trophy. He did not win by handling better or quartering the ground mechanically. He certainly did not win by retrieving. He won by finding and pointing more birds than his competition. When Trooper did not find birds, I could reasonably conclude that there were few to be found.

Now, one of the few advantages of living in Washington, D.C., is that somebody in town knows what went wrong with practically anything you can name. I, for example, can tell you how much better off the world would be if the people who made foreign policy would just listen to my advice. But for pheasants, I called a friend in the Fish and Wildlife Service. He told me that they were still moderately abundant in the very middle of the country: an arc from southern Minnesota through South Dakota, Iowa, Nebraska, and Kansas. West of the plains, hunting was good in places, but far down from historic levels. The eastern part of the country—from New England through Michigan and on south—was the worst. At this writing, the situation remains much the same. We may have had a continental total of more than 30 million pheasants in the autumn of 1986.[2] That is quite a few birds, but perhaps no more than were present in the Dakotas alone in the 1940s.

The problem is people: hunters, antihunters, developers, and farmers—most of whom are doing the wrong things. We made pheasant habitat and then we unmade it.

Habitat in the Middle-Land

The pheasant is an indicator species, like the brown trout. Both are clever, tough and adaptable. When either disappears, something may be happening that is not good for humans either. Both are able to thrive in rural areas—the middle-land between cities and wilderness. These are the areas where we produce our food and, for the most part, where we go for outdoor recreation.

Ask a biologist why pheasants are declining. In most cases, he will tell you that the leading problem is deterioration of habitat. The hedgerows have been torn out, creating big, "clean" fields—clean of wildlife. The farm has turned into the Foxcroft Meadows Towne Houses, the woodlot into lawn, the pheasants into toy windmills with plastic wings spinning in the breeze.

Birds like the pheasant and bobwhite are emotionally elusive. They are wild and in that sense natural. Like all game, however, they can be harvested. Unlike some game, they are for the most part harvested on farms. They can be eradicated, or produced in very high numbers, or left to scratch out a living around the edges. They respond to the farmer's decisions almost as readily as does the alfalfa that feeds the cows that produce the milk that you and I drink. What will happen will be what the farmer wants. He has ideas of his own on the subject, but in the long term he will respond to the market, and to government regulators. The market is you and me. The people who elect governments are you and me. Our leaders are responsive to their electorate, so we get what the majority wants and deserve what we get.

We have no policy for the middle-land—or rather a series of conflicting policies run by competing agencies. Things don't have to be this way. The Europeans are land-poor and know it. They have few national parks and wilderness areas, but they have policies to avoid urban sprawl. They are used to the compromise between purity and civilization. In America we seem able to save virgin wilderness; unwilling to save the good places near where we live. We destroy our cities and, rather than rebuild them, move into the farm country around them. It is the urban equivalent of slash-and-burn agriculture.

Rural blight is not reversible after houses have replaced fields. As long as there are still farms and open spaces, however, we can improve habitat. A young organization called Pheasants Forever provides advice and helps to get local resources working on local habitat problems. It works. When we give Montana pheasants good winter cover and then refrain from mowing all the nesting hens with the alfalfa crop, there are birds around in the fall.

I would like to end the chapter here. Everyone loves nature, and habitat is nature's clothing. Good protective cover for pheasants is, therefore, good protective cover for writers. I recall a saying of Henry Kissinger's: "Don't collect enemies." The rest of the chapter may collect a few. Unfortunately, habitat is not quite the whole problem.

On the East Coast, pheasant cover is in trouble—no doubt about that—but some of the remaining good-looking places are lifeless too. There are abandoned farms near Ithaca, New York, that looked better in the 1980s than they did in the 1950s. Montana pheasants would love that cover. But in 1953 I got a dozen New York pheasants with no dog, and in 1989 the birds were gone.

Chemicals

Pesticides have been known to harm pheasant populations since at least the 1930s, when orchards in the northwest were sprayed with solutions of arsenic and lead. In 1946, farmers began to spray "DDT and organic poisons developed for chemical warfare . . . killing many pheasants."[3] More recently, organophosphate pesticides have been found in laboratory tests to be "extremely toxic to birds and mammals, fish, aquatic organisms and bees. . . . The Fish and Wildlife Service has documented several cases of wildlife killed by" organophosphates.[4] Studies proving wildlife poisoning, however, are expensive and rarely conducted. Typically the birds just get scarce and no one is quite sure of the reasons.

Direct poisoning of pheasants may not be as important as the effect of pesticides on food and cover. When insecticides work, they kill insects. Pheasant chicks depend upon insects for their first five or six weeks. "Recent work has shown that brood sizes increased dramatically where pesticide-free [field] margins were maintained."[5] Herbicides kill plants, some of which pheasants of all ages need for cover. Farmers increasingly dislike sprays too, but they must make a living. It is not easy. We need to give them incentives not to spray, and the demand for organic food may provide a chance. A report by the National Academy of Sciences finds that "farmers who apply little or no chemicals to crops are usually as productive as those who use pesticides and synthetic fertilizers, and . . . recommended changing Federal subsidy programs that encourage use of agricultural chemicals."[6]

Predators

Beasts of prey are theses and antitheses, symbols red in tooth and claw. Once they were evil: Predation took food from the mouths of hungry people. We are bloated now and need predators as a diet for the mind. The person who did most to raise our consciousness may have been Aldo Leopold,[7] a conservationist who was, I guess, my favorite nature writer since Thoreau. He made us aware of the predators' role in the balance of nature. Balance and nature: Surely there must be virtue in the conjunction of two such values. The goodness of predation became gospel to every enlightened environmentalist. Children today know that the bloody part of nature's way saves mankind from smifflication by mice. Our fanged friends add piquancy to television programs. My personal favorites are the raptors, who turn the living-room window into a nature-screen. Harriers and eagles and owls are worth watching no matter how often I see them. When the occasional big falcon skims by, I soar with it. Perhaps it is a peregrine, returned from the grave.

But then I talk to farmers. The pheasant population depends mainly on them—not on me, the hunter; not on departments of wildlife; not on biologists. There will be pheasants to hunt only if farmers in large numbers restore the necessary conditions. There is nothing philosphical about this. It is an economic decision. Farmers reckon that their job is to raise what you and I want: wheat (instead of thistles), carrots (instead of gophers), sheep (instead of coyotes), and sometimes pheasants (instead of things that eat pheasants). The whole point of farming is to alter nature's balance.

On the last day of last season, having flushed five cocks and missed every one of them, David King and I stopped at the farmhouse and took careful aim at the cookies. The folks told us that we would have seen far more birds in the sixties.

We asked what had gone wrong. Pesticicides?

No, thought our host. As compared to the chemicals used in the sixties, the new ones are less toxic and more expensive.

Habitat destruction?

Our host saw few changes on his own place. The pheasant cover is in stream-bottoms and draws that cannot be farmed.

What, then?

Well, there are far more predators. The raptors have come back under protection of the law. Coyotes, foxes, raccoons, and skunks increased when fur prices dropped and poisons were banned. Our host told us of digging up a fox's den in June and finding the remains of about twenty pheasants inside. Most of the dead birds were hens. At that time of the year, they would have been nesting.

It seems that the economic predator of the farmer clashes with the philosophic predator of us nature watchers. Let us turn to the biologist as a referee. Surely he, Leopold's child, agrees that predators have little impact on game populations.

Biology has moved on: "Recent studies have substantiated that predation is the leading cause of pheasant mortality, and that there has been an upward trend in hen mortality due to predation over the last three decades."[8] Predation is "a major factor influencing nesting success,"[9] as my farmer-host suspected. The red fox, great horned owl, and red-tailed hawk are the most important predators (but there may be others worth study). A "multispecies predator-control program could be a highly effective way to increase pheasants. . . ."[10]

Mind you, it is the deterioration of habitat that has exposed pheasants to their predators. Pheasants in good cover can thrive despite predation. But most habitat is not good today. Where it offers marginal protection, predators add to the stresses on populations that are already in trouble.

So. First I had to abandon the evil predator of childhood, the one that made me feel so cozy when Mom pulled the comforter around my ears. Never mind; the antithetical good predator was almost as satisfactory, in his wimpy way. Now he too is letting me down. The latest predator is neither invariably good nor bad but complicated, as syntheses have a way of being. This whole nature business is getting to be too much like foreign affairs.

If my living were threatened by coyotes overfond of mutton, I would have no conceptual problem whatever. No. I would have a varmint rifle in my pickup. As a writer, however, I get more sustenance from live predators than dead ones. They present the only issue in this chapter that is really fun. Clearly, then, I can afford to be philosophical. Here goes:

". . . one kills in order to have hunted" (Ortega y Gasset)[11]
"One eats in order to have killed" (Proper).
The meal is "meat from God" (Leopold).

Well now, gopher goulash is all right, but surely God does not mean for me to eat fricassee of fox?

U s

At core, the hunter's problem is that he is squeezed between a growing population and a shrinking resource. In the early eighties a friend who had been managing game in Pennsylvania told me that the state had "about 1,400,000 hunters, and that's a million too many" (for the land available). He was right, if one assumes that hunting in America will continue to be managed as it has in the past, with game as a low priority. But in some small European countries there is game. Sometimes it is abundant. It is there because people want it enough to pay for it.

When pheasants and trout grew scarce in America, our first step was to demand that fish-and-game departments raise more and turn them loose. It seemed obvious. It was done. It failed, and in the process it squandered the sparse resources that hunters had contributed when they bought their licenses and paid taxes on their equipment.

There is a place for stocked trout in put-and-take fishing and a place for stocked pheasants on shooting preserves. Using them to boost wild populations is clearly poor practice. In Montana, research showed that stocking made fishing worse by damaging wild trout populations. Biologists now conclude that wild pheasant populations can be harmed by the release of pen-raised birds.[12] I believe it. I have seen released birds attracting predators and found stocked pheasants infested with parasites. If they carry those, perhaps they also carry disease. They indisputably carry genes, and some biologists are extremely concerned about the introduction of inferior genes into wild populations.

So we circle back yet again to good habitat. It is not the only problem, but it is the most basic. Habitat needs to be rebuilt on very large areas, not just little patches here and there. It will cost money. Who pays?

The Endangered Species

In early October, John Bietenduefel and I asked two Montana farmers what they had in mind for opening day.

"I'm going to hide in the cellar," said Lyle.

"Cellar's not deep enough," said Dick.

Farmers worry most about deer-hunters: They use rifles, and rifle bullets carry a long way. On the other hand, farmers often need hunters to control booming deer populations. I have had farmers tell me that I could go bird-hunting only if I would promise to come back and shoot a doe when deer season opened.

No farmer has ever asked me to help him get rid of the pesky pheasants—and after deer-hunters, opening-day pheasant-hunters draw the most complaints. They come from distant cities in large, sociable groups. Some farmers turn away cars with out-of-county license plates. Others reject hunters from big cities (especially Butte, in the case of Montana). Still other farmers say that they would like to blame strangers, but that in fact local boys cause more problems.

The complaints are even more varied than the screening mechanisms. There are the open gates, the fields with tire tracks, the damaged crops, the signs with holes shot in them, the spooked horses, the road-hunting, the time wasted by once-a-year glad-handing, the pheasants just "breasted out" and tossed away. The farmer asks: "Why did they shoot 'em if they didn't want 'em?" He would have liked to hunt those birds himself—and eat them. He admits that the hunters who give offense are a minority, but not a minority small enough to be passed off as "the bad one percent."

This is not pleasant to hear. Having spent some few years as a political reporter, however, I have slipped into the bad habit of listening to both sides of an argument; and having accepted the hospitality of farmers, I feel obliged to write down what they have said. Their image of the hunter is distressingly different from the hunter's image of the hunter.

Beneath the farmers' complaints, there seems to be a deeper problem: The freedom that American hunters consider a right is, from the farmers' point of view, one-sided. He sees the hunters as taking without giving back. The unequal deal mattered little when there were many farmers and few hunters. Today, farmers feel like an endangered species. Many have come to look on hunters as a no-win proposition: at a minimum, nuisances; at a maximum, causes of financial loss. There are farmers who have destroyed game habitat so as not to be bothered.

If we want pheasants, we will have to show farmers that there is something in the deal for them. The change is already being imposed by that relentless American decision-maker, the market. Some of the bigger farms are making money from game. Pheasants, however, have from the beginning been every man's game in this country, and some of those who are unwilling or unable to pay are deeply angered by the trend. They are seeing the end of one more frontier, one more of the good things that made America different from a decadent old world.

There is a fundamental conflict in two of our old guiding principles: first, that the public owns game; and second, that the landowner controls access to the game. I have no intention of trying to reconcile the irreconcilable. I just want pheasants.

The years in Europe were sobering. ("You are what you eat," somebody said, but I'm where I've lived.) Before 1973, Portugal had superb partridge-hunting, perhaps even better than that in Spain. The climate was right and pheasant-farming maintained excellent habitat. Pressure increased as more people acquired automobiles and shotguns, but lands leased and managed for game insured good breeding reserves. Hunting was best on the leases but still good on property nearby where permission could be had for the asking. Birds, it seems, fly over fences without reading the signs.

Then came the revolution. One of the "demands of the people" was the right to hunt anywhere, without asking permission. The new government granted the demand. Everybody exercised it. My friends and I got stuck for hours in a traffic jam of hunters driving back to Lisbon after opening day. I walked up and down the lines of tiny cars so full of hunters and dogs that heads were sticking out of windows. It seemed inconceivable that, in a country so small and poor, so many people who knew nothing of the sport would put up with so much discomfort for it.

But of course there was no longer an incentive to manage land for game, and no one did. The partridges were gone after a couple of seasons. Next to go were the old-world quail and snipe. Everybody got his share, and then one day there was nothing left.

Perhaps we have enough land on these shores to use some of it for gentlemen's sport. If that creates good habitat, a few pheasants may just leak over the edges for my kind of sport, too.

The Winter Hatch

There is one charge of which we hunters can be absolved. If we shoot only cocks—as the law usually requires—we do not harm pheasant populations. Farmers are often unaware of this. They ought to be, because every farmyard used to have chickens. For maximum production, farmer's wives did not keep six hens and six cocks. They kept perhaps ten hens and one cock. That is a conservative breeding ratio for pheasants, too. A single rooster can fertilize the eggs of twenty hens without complaint. "He lives for springtime," as an Irish friend used to say.

It is "virtually impossible to overhunt cock pheasants."[13] Hen survival may even improve when some of the big, tough cocks are removed from competition for scarce late-winter food and shelter. For at least a century, British and European gamekeepers have recommended the removal of surplus cocks.[14] (Lord knows I try.)

Writer Ted Trueblood once joked about the miraculous appearance of cock pheasants after the end of hunting season. He called it "the winter hatch" of roosters. The real explanation is that pheasants have an unsual way of escape: perhaps an adaptation to living with men for centuries. Under pressure, the cock does not keep coming back to the same "lie," like a trout, or even to the same covert like a ruffed grouse. He moves out of the neighborhood till things cool down. He moves to posted land, roadside ditches, back yards, and other off-limits areas. When you and I stop hunting, he moves back, with his cohort: the winter hatch.

So pheasants are, after all, not extinct, not endangered, and not even as scarce as you might think if you keep on hunting in the good old ways of the good old days. You have to hunt where they are, first, and that is the subject of the next chapter. Then you have to be smarter than a rooster, which is the subject of the following chapter. It is not as easy as it sounds. They're real pheasants now.

8

✦

Intelligence

During the next week, Trooper and I healed all six feet while I applied my head to the problem. That dog was a great recuperator. From Sunday through Wednesday he slept under the kitchen counter, except when my wife rolled him over and reminded him that he ought to go out and kill some shrubbery. By Thursday he was up in the morning and asking if I was headed for the office or someplace worthwhile. By Saturday he could make a standing long-jump into the rear of the wagon. And by then I was ready for some head-hunting, which was intended to work better than foot-hunting.

I pretended to be in Ireland. Irish birds cope with a paucity of good protective cover, fields grazed bare, and 5 million Irishmen devoted to roast pheasant. Sounds like parts of America in the bad new days. In Ireland my friends had concerned themselves with intelligence, so that is how Trooper and I set about doing it to the recently scarce pheasants of the New World. We could hardly do worse than we had by roaming where a free spirit beckoned.

By "intelligence," I do not refer to the brain cells, though Trooper had those, too. (For instance, he had quickly perceived that pheasant tastes good, and nothing would persuade him that it was wrong to have a little chew.) No, by intelligence I mean the kind of information collected by the Department of Dirty Tricks about our opponents overseas. In the easy old days, my approach had been to get hunting permission in several places before the season, then hunt wherever it felt good. It worked when there were lots of birds and few hunters, but not vice versa.

In Ireland, Ned Maguire would tell me of a conversation with Mrs. Murphy after the Mass. She had heard a cock crowing during a picnic at Roundwood. Right: Let's get the dog and have a look. Sometimes we found what we were looking for. We never found more than one, but chasing it was more fun than shooting an easy limit, and more meritorious. You do not want to shoot many of the clever ones. Inflation depreciates the currency of emotion.

The Irish gave me a new way of looking at brown trout, gray partridges, and red grouse; and no Irishman was ever heard to suggest that pheasants occupy a lower pedestal than any of these. At the Irish dinner table, the pheasant sits above the salt with the woodcock. An old cock pheasant is, perhaps, the toughest to hunt of the lot.

It did not hurt that the Irish shared my passion for pointing dogs—which they considered the most practical way to convey bird from hedgerow to table. Trooper was not with me there, but we'd turn loose Ned's English setter, Paddy's Irish setter, Bryan's dropper (pointer-setter cross), or Liam's shorthair. The dog would take a quick run around all four sides of a field. We'd wait and, if the dog came back, go through the gate to the next field, and the next, and a dozen more. We'd hike five miles while the pointer ran fifty and found the pheasant that someone had told us to look for in one of them. When the point came, the fellow who was not the handler (me) would discover that he could, after all, get through a hedge made for turning dairy bulls. I'd get more scratches than birds. Still, during the season, the rope in the coal shed usually had something hanging from it, aging: a pheasant.

One cock pheasant.

Singular Hunting

The idea is not to look for pheasants, plural and abstract, but pheasant: a singular, particular, concrete cock pheasant. You have to find them one by one, not collectively. Consider it a kind of big-game hunting—not a ridiculous comparison, these days. While pheasants were decreasing, deer were increasing, and now I can usually shoot one for venison in an hour or so. A good buck still takes intelligence, and so does a cock pheasant.

You might spot one from your car, especially early and late in the days before the season opens. Take binoculars. The cock is not as wary of cars as of people on foot, but he is more shy than he was in 1945 or 1969. You will do better exploiting his tragic flaw: He talks too much. The cackling decreases, but does not cease, as the days get shorter. It goes on even during the late season. Mostly the rooster brags to the neighborhood in early morning and late evening, when hunters are drinking coffee or putting ointment on blisters. He is most likely to blow his cover one-half hour before sunrise. If you are listening, you can wait till the legal shooting time, then go out and amputate his reveille.

Of course, if you live two hours' drive from the hunting, arrival before sunrise means getting up early in the morning, or perhaps late at night. You could talk instead to the fellow who lives there: the farmer. He, as you might expect, knows something about musical performances on his acres. He may share the knowledge—and the hunting—with a solitary hunter who looks as if he can be counted on to stay out of standing crops. Farmers are extra-wary of hunters who come by the van-load.

During that Pennsylvania November, one farmer told me that he had heard a cock crowing behind the house the evening before. I stepped into the field carelessly, figuring that the bird had moved on, and flushed it within ten feet. Pheasants love dirty tricks. This one found out that I can shoot my old double 12-gauge pretty fast. On the other hand, a repeater might have allowed me to miss five times instead of two, earning some sort of award for nonexploitative use of the environment.

At least the intelligence was good.

Where They Aren't

In heavily hunted country you may be surprised, on the dawn patrol, to find how many pretty places have no cocks. Trooper and I almost stopped hunting on land that was not posted—my favorite old coverts. In places where hunters could just jump out of their cars and get going, the birds departed early in the season and did not return till it was over. I had no special private access but spent some time knocking on doors. It was much less fun than hunting. I felt like an encyclopedia salesman, but encyclopedia salesmen presumably sell the occasional encyclopedia. I got permission to hunt in the occasional place that had birds.

When the Pennsylvania season ended, Trooper and I went south of the Mason-Dixon line, into Maryland, and hunted for six more weeks. It was a pattern that we had followed for years. In 1982, however, we found more pheasants south of Pennsylvania for the first time. Maryland had become, in effect, all posted property. A new law made it illegal to hunt except by written permission from the landowner—with high fines and no excuses. It hurt. Then it improved the sport. What impressed me most was the discovery that Mennonite farms had no pheasants even in Maryland. The Mennonites, bless their souls, would sign anybody's permission slip, and everybody knew it, including the pheasants, which moved out.

Posted signs meant the end of hunting in the free old way. I'd rather take a trip in back in time than anywhere else, but the change saved hunting near Washington. Most of us hunters thought of the problem as finding birds. The bigger problem was escaping from people.

Cover

But there was still the matter of hunting in the right cover, because cocks were nowhere abundant, and they did not spend all day at the site of their reveille.

One of the most useful bits of intelligence was that pheasants were no longer in standing corn. Hunters have been slow to cope with this atrocity. Pheasants and corn used to go together like apple pie and cheese, love and marriage, horse and carriage. The biggest losers have been hunters without dogs, who could flush birds from corn more easily than from most other cover. I do not mean that pheasants now dislike corn: they feed on broken ears lying around after harvesting, and before that they run into standing corn when pushed. But they do not dawdle there. The problem seems to be that herbicides have killed off the grass and weeds in "no-till" corn. It was the undergrowth that pheasants used to like, more than the tall stalks. Check a cornfield in the snow now and see how scarce tracks are. Even the mice have left.

Half a dozen farmers gave me the same story: They had just harvested forty acres of corn (or thirty, or a hundred) and hardly a pheasant had flown out of it. Bobwhites were even more scarce. Pheasants were still around, but less of them, and elsewhere.

Elsewhere turned out to be big fields—the bigger the better— ungrazed and overgrown. Call it grass, in shorthand. More precisely, it is herbacous cover: grasses, forbs, legumes, annuals with lots of seeds. Later in the eighties, the Conservation Reserve Program would give us the best of all: fields of tall, stiff grasses that would not mat down even in the winter. But there were some good places even in 1982. Old, unmown hayfields were best.

Stream-bottoms and swamps were worth hunting too, but not quite as good. This may seem surprising. Wet cover is where most hunters go when the birds get scarce, but then most hunters do not have pointing dogs. Pheasants want to be (1) where the hunter is not and (2) where he will have trouble cornering them if he follows. Swamps may have edges of some kind where the bird can be forced to fly: edges where reeds meet water or cattails meet thinner cover. In a big field with the right cover, a cock can dodge a human forever without being herded to an edge.

Pheasants prefer ground-cover of a certain density. (Always have, I suppose, though the corn fooled us.) Inside, they want tunnellike paths just big enough for an agile bird. A dog (or a fox) is taller, so he has to waste energy pushing through heavy vegetation. A hawk cannot see down through it. A cock pheasant, however, can jump out with one push of those springy legs. He likes that better than brush that tangles his wings. (I have seen him get stuck).

Ideally, the cover should come somewhere between a hunter's knee and his waist. Of course you have seen pheasants in lower stuff. Wouldn't surprise me to hear that a cock had escaped unseen across a billiard table, but he'd rather improve the odds.

During the rest of the three-month season, Trooper got me a pheasant every Saturday. One would have been more than enough to make the world fit to live in for the rest of the week. It was hard to convince Trooper that we should quit in the morning, though, so most Saturdays we wound up with our limit of two by sundown. Two cocks are almost an embarrassment of riches. I would have felt better hiding them and pretending that we had been skunked. For proper aging, however, birds must cool and dry quickly. The only place with good air circulation was the top of Trooper's mesh cage.

Trucks on the interstate highway would slow down while drivers peered inside the station wagon at those birds. The boys from the service station would stand around, hoping that I would reveal the hot spot. My wagon's odometer was going around for the second time, but the folks in new Mercedes had to wait while my windshield was washed and my oil checked twice.

If you want to find what pheasants mean to the American

people, try carrying a couple of them around in full feather one January day. It is like traveling in July with a very pretty lady wearing less plumage. Observe. You, personally, are invisible, because everyone is watching your symbol. You want to know what the real national bird is? It's not the bald eagle, nor yet Benjamin Franklin's wild turkey. The people have chosen. They vote with South Dakota.

9

✦

Three Pheasants

Pheasant hunters can be counted upon for advice that is eager, sincere, and conflicting. Most of it is accurate. The birds live in tall cover and short, run far and sit tight, flush wild and wait till stepped on, give easy shots and are impossible to hit. Hunters have responded in different ways, each of which has created a different pheasant of the mind.

The ways are:

1. Fishing
2. Hunting with a flushing dog
3. Hunting with a pointing dog

There is yet a fourth pheasant if one heeds the folks for whom it threatens the American way of life.

The confusion arises because some of those who cherish one pheasant are barely aware of others. Tactical advice does not help when it comes from the hunter of a different bird.

The Fisherman's Pheasant

Most of us start without a bird dog, or with Rover. Rover trees squirrels, chases rabbits, shares life. On pheasants, Rover turns out to be part of the problem rather than part of the solution. We have to find birds on our own.

It works when they are abundant, and preferably innocent. Abundance is still possible on opening day in good pheasant country. Innocence is not so easy to measure. On the average, about seventy percent[1] of the birds are young of the year, on opening day, meaning that they have never been shot at—but their fathers probably were. Males that were not adapted to the demands of the shotgun have been removed from the gene pool for up to a hundred generations, which is more than enough to change a species' habits. Still, a portion of the young cocks will have no better sense than to flush just because you are walking by. When someone tells you that pheasants are easy, these are the ones he means. They aren't the real thing. Sometimes I have had the courage to stay home on opening day.

Linear cover provides another chance. Hunters without dogs learn to walk hedgerows, one man on each side, stopping often to probe thick spots. It worked till thick hedgerows fell victim to modern farming. The skinny ones that I have hunted in recent years have been used mostly by commuters—birds getting from one cover to another by the least-bad route. Most have flown before I could get in range. ("Flushing wild," we call that. It might make a good title for a novel.)

There are other coverts that concentrate birds in small areas: limestone "rock breaks" in the middle of a Maryland field, for example, covered by sumac and briars and poison ivy; or shelterbelts in Montana. Snow tends to concentrate pheasants. It leaves a minimum of secure cover, and they feel visible in some of that, so many they flush easily. Further, they leave tracks. You hope that these will lead you to the bird that made them. They do not, usually, but they let you know that one is around. If the tracks are large, you know that it is a cock. You will hear that you can spot a rooster by the marks of its long tail feathers, but do not count on it. Pheasants try to hold their tails up.

If you hunt with a group, you can work larger coverts by organizing a drive. The stronger hunters are the drivers. They form a moving line that pushes pheasants toward hidden, quiet blockers. This is maneuver more than chase; shooting more than hunting. It makes for a social occasion, the kind of thing you can do Thanksgiving morning with once-a-year gunners. Driving the cornfields is an innocent memory of the fifties and sixties. After that, farmers lost patience with hunters knocking down standing corn, and anyhow the pheasants left it. But there are, here and there, other coverts with enough birds to make driving worthwhile.

Under most circumstances, a man without a dog is fishing—working what looks like a good place and hoping that something will turn up. The problem is that species like pheasants and brown trout get too clever for this. When you want a good brown, you scout the stream till you see one feeding, and then you aim your fly at it. That's hunting. You may get an eager brown by chuck-and-chance-it fishing, at random, and you might get an opening-day pheasant by throwing rocks in brushpiles, but that's fishing too.

Fishing is an act of faith.

Hunting is sensory.

A pheasant fisherman can learn much of nature and his game. He can learn the weedy clumps on south slopes where birds go for winter sunshine, learn where they feed in morning and evening, learn where they rest at noon, learn where they fly to roost. But the educated birds do not follow a routine—any routine. Routine, for a cock pheasant, is the equivalent of Wild Bill Hickock sitting with his back to a door. Wild Bill Pheasant has only one dependable habit: He makes himself scarce when he hears you coming. Sometimes he flies, but mostly he runs. You do not even know that the pheasant *used* to be there. Pheasant senses man; man does not sense pheasant.

How, then, can you hunt? Well, you cannot, but a dog can. He has the right sensor. His nose knows. He is the hunter and you are his equerry. In Huckleberry's first full season, when he was a year old, my friends and I shot about sixty wild cocks in his company; and of these I recall only one that we found before he did. He was trailing a different bird on the far side of a stream-bottom. I took a shortcut through the thick stuff, saw a patch of snowberry bushes shaking, and jumped almost on top of a cock. Score: Huckleberry 59, fishermen 1.

By now you may be thinking, if you have no dog, that sure, it's easy for those who do. It's not, though. It's more demanding, just as hunting for brown trout is more difficult than casting where you will. You have to train your dog, which means training yourself. If you choose a pointing dog, you must abandon most of what you think you know about hunting and learn it over from him. Flushing dogs are less complicated.

The Flushing Dog's Pheasant

The flushing dog is bred to do just that: push birds into the air as soon as he finds them, rather than waiting for his human to do it. Clearly, then, the flusher must work close to the gun. This means that the area covered is limited, and even then you have little time to get ready for shots. (In all of this, I am writing of real pheasants, not the pen-raised kind. You can hunt them with any good dog and find most shots easy.)

Some hunters train their flushing dogs to sit at a whistled command. (Voice commands can cause wild flushes.) Such training is a substitute for the pointing instinct, but unlike the point it goes against the dog's nature, which raises complications both in the teaching and in hunting. Of the dog/man team, the human is the one who knows least about what the bird is doing and is therefore least qualified to call a halt. Most of my friends take an easier way out, counting on rapport with the dog to minimize wild flushes. Rapport should be the flushing dog's strong point. He may, when he learns what you want, give you some warning before he gets the bird up. Golden retrievers have a way of crawling on their bellies when they hit hot scent. You might even find a flushing dog that looks back to get your permission (though field-trial rules say that he should not hesitate).

Groups

A flushing dog may fit easily into your old group of human companions. Most of them will keep on fishing as they always have, working to the end of hedgerows, probing brush, beating the cover. The flusher's nose-to-the-ground method is compatible. The pointer's method, on the contrary, seems intuitively wrong to untrained humans. The pointing dog checks patches of cover with a quick pass. He uses air scent, which to you is shapeless, invisible, worse than nebulous, counterintuitive. You hack at the dog to come back and be more careful. You persist in fishing out a visually attractive place that ought to have a pheasant. The pointer's nose knows better. He concludes that the humans do not need him and that he does not need the humans. And then he goes off to find a bird by himself. You tell yourself that next time you'll get a closer-working dog.

Sometimes the group will want to arrange a drive. Its geometry will be human, incomprehensible to any dog. The pointer will chase birds in the wrong direction or point them in some thick patch of cover, out of sight. He is very likely to spoil the maneuver. The flusher may at least stay close to his boss. Retrievers in particular are bred to be good at heeling until they are needed for finding downed birds. Pointers can and should be trained to stay at heel, too. They like it a little better than vivisection.

Perhaps your friends will shoot rabbits. That's all in a day's work, for a close-ranging flusher. If a wide-ranging pointing dog decides that rabbits are fair game, he will chase them—and you will chase the dog. You will not find him easy to catch.

The Flushing Dog's Cover

If you know birds of prey, think of the flushing dog as a goshawk: short of wing, built for winding through trees at low altitude, then pouncing. It is a game of ambushes, not nerves; woods, not fields; ground, not air; boundaries, not horizons. I would love it if pointers had not spoiled me. It is a good game for pheasants when you play it in the right places.

The flusher's limited range is put to best use in:

- Cover that is limited in area, but with with many birds. (You do not need a pointer there, and he does not need the sensory overload.)
- Cover that is extremely dense, such as standing cattails. (A bird in there may refuse to be pinned by a pointer, sneaking off every time he approaches. The flusher gets the pheasant up before it can escape.)
- Cover that is too tall to see over and too thick to shoot through. (A dog that pushes the bird out does not necessarily get you more birds, but he saves you from wading into the jungle to honor a point.)

Oddly, there is less of such cover in the humid East than in the arid West. In the high desert, brush sprouts along every watercourse from the Missouri River to intermittent ditches. Fields too bare for a vole yield to thickets in which even ruffed grouse cannot fly. This is not the prettiest of cover to hunt: vegetation and tactics are both short on diversity. Lift up thine eyes unto the hills. Mountains on the horizon make up for the sameness of willow tangles. A flushing dog lets you enjoy the macroscenery while he explores the microhabitat. The birds are in there—and one of the best things about pheasant cover, after all, is pheasants. Irrigation is good for them. It exploits the basic wealth of land and sun. In the absence of soaking rain, chicks thrive. Brush shelters the birds in winter, hides them from predators, and may in some cases nourish them all year. George Kelly, who lives in the Bighorn Valley of Montana, tells me that he kills some cocks with nothing but stream-bottom seeds in their crops, even when other pheasants nearby are living on grain.

A Flushing Dog for the Uplands

Mr. Bugatti is rumored to have said, once, that his cars were made "to go, not to stop." If he was indeed responsible for that nonsense, he must have known that he was making excuses. A fast car with weak brakes is an accident waiting to happen. Flushing dogs do not come equipped with brakes, so they are not given fast bodies. Strains developed for water-work are likely to be heavy, thick-coated, and shaped for swimming rather than running. But there are upland strains too, and they produce good compromises. George Kelly's Jake, a Labrador, is one of them. He has the light weight of a pointer (fifty pounds) and a structure not much different. Spaniels are often built right if you get the little ones, under forty pounds. Avoid show strains like the plague. They were designed for gathering dust under sofas.

A merry springer will cover the ground at close range better than any other dog there is. He will be, moreover, as much fun to watch as a pointer—almost.

The Pointer's Pheasant

The pointer has brakes. When he locates a bird, he points it and lets you do the flushing. He can therefore be fast. His game is go and stop: contradictory elements that depend on each other, like love and death.

Almost everone who sees a pointer holding birds agrees on the beauty and practicality of the thing. Our ancestors spent centuries developing the trait, for good reason. Problems arise not in concept but execution. The most important thing in a dog, really, is its individual nature. A golden retriever that wants to help (and many do) is a far more comfortable companion than a pointer that wants to do its own thing (and too many of our American pointing dogs do). A spaniel that you can see gets you more shots than a pointer over the hills and far away. That much is fact.

What I have is bias: caught it in Tunisia from a belly-dancer built like a Chesapeake Bay retriever. We foreign guests were given front-row seats from which there was no escape. Dancer and guests wound up sweating in equal profusion. Do not, therefore, expect objectivity. For me, upland hunting without a pointer is emotional deprivation. Pointers are as good to watch as the prettiest dancer in the Cork Ballet Company. Fortunately, she can cook, and my pointer can find birds. Both of them seem to like my company.

The pointer creates a pheasant as exciting as the fly-fisher's trout. We usually start fishing with worms (and should, in my view). When we become more committed—willing to learn something more difficult—we drift to the fly rod and pointer. We claim to get more trout and birds afterwards. That, however, is citing practical results to explain wildly impractical pursuits. We are really chasing something of the mind.

MOMENTS: Fly floats on bright water; trout drifts up. Dog catches scent in midair, lands curved and tense.
CONFLICT: Fly is delicate, trout wary, their meeting violent. Pointer bends the grass like a squall, stands like a snowdrift. Catches bird in desire, body innocent.
MYTH: Books, tales, history, art, science, magic, feathers, and the code.

Still, commitment is a bother when one lacks time for it. No dog can be shut in the closet for nine months like a fishing rod. A flushing dog may, at least, spend those months without much attention and still show you some birds when the season comes. A pointer is the kind of high-risk investment that needs attention if it is not to go sour. On the other hand, it is capable of producing high gains.

The Force-Multiplier

The pointer is A Faulcon towring in her pride of place, a longwing as her lovers call her, a wide circle about your center, a medieval relic who stoops to conquer. Granted that she is not needed where pheasants abound. Given few birds and short cover, it helps to have a dog that can do ten miles to her human's one. She not only finds birds that you would miss, like other dogs, but vastly expands your range. She is a force-multiplier as well as a sensor. Watch while she checks every objective in a twenty-acre field, then looks back to ask where both of you are going to have fun next. If you are not smiling by then, this is the wrong sport for you.

Learn to forget geometry. You are a seeing and reasoning human, imprisoned by Euclid. Your world is straight lines of grain, curving hedgerows, points of cover, planes of field, parallel rows of drivers. The pointer seeks eddies and splotches of scent. If there is a wash of pheasant in the air, he slows and looks for more, then works on it. If there is no scent, he moves on. Move with him. Accept "reason's insufficiency," as Ortega y Gasset says, placing another animal between your reason and the game.[2]

Remember at least this much: Your dog does not hunt birds. He hunts scent.

Sure Shots

Pointing dogs give you some shots that you might find embarrassingly easy. Of course, you could wait till the bird gets almost out of range. Not me. My average on pheasants is worse than it is on partridges and doves. Maybe it's just that the smaller birds provide more practice. Maybe it is that I have no great trouble missing anything that flies. When the dog manages to hold a cock till it can be shot at modest range, I am grateful.

The opera needs violence, but let's make the last act a short one. Men used to set up long, tough shots on pheasants. They used to play trout till they turned belly-up, too. Those were sporting opportunities—for humans. I want to give the cock a better death than he might get from other predators. Call it a deal: I deprive him of time, spare him from being eaten alive. He would not take the deal if he had a choice, but it's the best I can offer. The cat playing with a captured bird does not know compassion, but you and I should. Let's get the trout in the net and the pheasant in the game-pocket quickly.

The Pointer's Cover

Wide, grassy fields create pheasants that the hunter without a dog should probably avoid. They will run out of his path and then sit tight. Flushing dogs find the birds and give you shots, if game is abundant. If there is only one cock in a hundred acres, the flusher will be slow to locate it and may then push it up out of gunshot range, unless stopped by command.

A look at any predator's body will tell you the kind of cover that it was designed for. In Africa, there is a cat so odd that the Portuguese mistakenly called it a "deerlike wolf"—*lobo cerval*. That translates into English as "serval." You find it in fields of grass, hunting francolins and hares. In America, such cover would have pheasants, prairie grouse, and jackrabbits (our versions of the hare). The serval looks like a pointer, light in bone, long of leg.

Anthropologists puzzle over the pressures that could force a four-footed ape to stand up. Open fields would certainly make me want to do it. Herbaceous cover grows where a dog lives. In warm weather, it is inferno for a heavy-bodied, short-legged breed, tough on any dog. The grasses and forbs wear out his legs, exhaust his lungs, redden his eyes, push little burrs between his toes, big burrs into his coat, awns everywhere. These guardians of the pheasant account for my use of leggy, wiry dogs with short coats—like a serval.

It is a matter of levels. Ruffed grouse cover is young jungle, thickest at about the level of my eye, forcing me to bob and weave and parry. I love it but my erect body was not designed for it, so I think of it as hard going. The same trees shade out ground cover, however, making movement as easy for my dog as it is difficult for me. Any dog in good condition can hunt woods grouse, day after day—the problem being to hold birds that have few places to hide. Pheasants in the grass can hide anywhere, and do. There is no cover in which they feel so cozy.

Herding

The word "strategy" is often shrunk to describe a tactic. Herding is a real pheasant-hunting strategy, however. It works for all pheasants of the mind, with variations. This mnemonic device will help to remember it: Bow toward mecca. Mecca is where you wish to shoot your pheasant.

You reply that you like to shoot pheasants *anywhere*. Ah, but you cannot. You cannot, for example, shoot one that flushes behind opaque brush. Don't herd toward that.

You will be told to herd from thick cover toward thin. This is good advice, if you have no dog, because the pheasant is likely to flush when it reaches cover where it might be seen: low stubble, for instance. Unfortunately, it may also run fifty yards into the thin stuff and then flush wild. If you have a flushing dog, therefore, you may prefer to herd toward heavy cover (so long as you can still see over it). The bird will be more difficult to flush—but more likely to be in range when it does.

The pointing dog gives a solitary hunter maximum scope for strategy. There are three reasons for this:

- First, a dog that points (rather than flushing) naturally tends to herd birds. In the days before guns, fowlers sometimes used pointers for driving birds into a net.
- Second, pheasants (being reluctant to flush) are perhaps the most vulnerable of our game birds to herding. Their weakness coincides with the pointer's strength. It says something about the cultural bias of American hunters that, instead of turning the pheasant's behavior to our advantage, we traditionally complain about "skulking."
- Third, the pointer's mecca—and yours—are the same: the big, grassy fields.

Trooper was a "high-couraged old pointer,"[3] hardened to the pilgrimages. One of them fell on the Saturday before Christmas holidays, in Maryland. We were hunting behind a party of three other hunters with two dogs, so we limped toward evening without a feather in the game pocket. I was limping, at least. As a hunter I have fewer talents than most dogs but I do have long legs, toes that point straight forward, and a disposition to follow them till the matter of Christmas dinner has been settled.

Trooper was still ranging, but it was near sundown when he went on point, off in the distance. Before I could get close, a covey of bobwhites flushed wild and passed me, almost out of range, headed for some second-growth woods. The earlier party had probably made them nervous. I took a shot with my gun's long-range left barrel and, while nothing fell, I thought that one bird landed too soon, in thick old hay at the edge of the woods. On the remote chance that it had been hit, I ran to the spot and asked Trooper to "hunt dead"—look for a dead bird. I stood still to avoid confusing the scent. Then, after a few minutes, I slumped on a limestone outcrop while Trooper kept looking for something to chew. When he stopped, his nose was pointing down at the ground. I walked in to pick up a dead seven-ounce quail and flushed a three-pound cock pheasant in excellent flying condition. With no time to think, I did not flinch and the bird came down to the right barrel. I raced Trooper to it, as usual, and found it before he could ruin a holiday dinner.

By now, it seemed clear to me that there was no bobwhite around, but Trooper did not want to leave the tall grass. Probably just wanted to enjoy his recent triumph: another of his defects. So I sagged onto the soft rock again. And Trooper pointed again. When I reached him he broke point, ran thirty yards, and pointed a second time. I trotted up and he went off fifty yards to a third point. Poor old dog had been running so long that his overheated brain was producing fantasies. But this time, when I circled in from the side, the fantasy jumped into the air and cackled off, setting sun glowing through fanned-out wing feathers.

Those two roosters chose to stay in the grass, not the woodlot; and they held despite walking, running, waiting, grass-kicking, shooting, cussing, whistle-blowing, bell-ringing, and dog-calling. All of it took place within a few yards of the birds—sometimes a few feet. The pheasants did not move till the dog gave them no choice.

We headed for the car with two birds the color of Christmas bulging my game pocket. Now both of us could afford to limp.

Part IV

Dogs

10

The
Pheasant's
Rules

Our ancestors dominated savage beasts by force of personality.
Intrepid Victorians stared down tigers in the jungle, lions on
the veldt, wolves on the tundra. That's as may be. My domesticated
wolf is more intrepid than me.

Huckleberry rests his head on the arm of my chair and gazes till
I look up from work to say (not very sternly) "now cut that out." He
does. Instead he wriggles his muzzle under my elbow and lets me
know that an ear-rub would be welcome. I rub with my right hand
and type with my left. Huck nibbles at a flea-suspect that turns out
to be the button on my sleeve. Then he runs to the vestibule and
brings me a boot, for which I pat him on the head. I do not want the
boot, but it is what he thinks I want, so I want him to think that I
want it. I am training him to fetch. This is how I encourage him.

On second thought, I do want the boot, and the one that goes with it. I put both of them on. Huck is training me to keep my priorities straight. He encourages me by standing upright and dancing around on crooked hind legs, like the god Pan. I disclaim responsibility for that trick; my wife is the dance teacher around this house.

Huckleberry wants to go hunting. He wants it because it is in his genes. I want it because it is in my genes. The hunting game makes no sense, these days, but it still feels as if it ought to.

We drive to a nearby public hunting area that turns out to have been heavily grazed. Birds could only have survived by moving into what Montanans think of as pheasant cover—anything cows cannot eat. It is just cattle noncover, but Huck is eighteen months old now and sure that he can find a pheasant anywhere. He runs with nose high along the line between cover too thick and cover too thin, a moon orbiting my earth.

In a half-acre patch of snowberries and wild roses, Huck sniffs at a pile of feathers from a bird killed, probably, on opening day. Then he casts around and leaves the brush without hunting it thoroughly. I resist the urge to call him back, remembering times in his short life when he has discovered a world invisible to me. He lopes across a bare field, tentative. In its middle he stands on his front legs and does the cactus-dance, hind feet in the air. It is the opposite of the Pan-dance. Huck can avoid prickly-pears with his front feet, but he has found that his hind feet do not track in exactly the same places, so up they come. He has also worked out a choreography for other things that hurt, such as porcupines and skunks. He wants to save time for what is good. He is on the trail of it. By now even a nose-blind human can tell.

Huck pushes through thick willows into the bottom of a slough cushioned with cattails. They are like the plush lining on the inside of a lady's purse. He trails another two-hundred yards, runs a broad loop to get the wind right, and works in my direction. Perhaps we can trap the bird between us. I lower my weapon and charge. The pheasant runs out of the bottom and through the willow screen, flushing on the far side. I cannot see it well enough to be sure that it is a legal cock rather than an illegal hen, so I do not shoot—but it is acting like a cock that knows about guns.

Huck comes to heel and I trot him in the direction the bird seemed to take. Three-hundred yards away, he finds its scent. He starts to stiffen, changes his mind, trails with two near-points, then points firmly at a clump of junipers. I try to get far enough in front but the pheasant, with no ground cover to hide in, runs out and flushes far from both of us. It is indeed a cock, red wattles rampant, snowy ring resplendent below evergreen head, orange breast aflame, tail pennants flouting the idiot with a shotgun. This pageantry of the chase streams off, almost out of sight. Just before it disappears, I think I see it flare its wings and tip back to land. I mark the spot and heel the pup to it as quickly as I can move without becoming too breathless to shoot.

This time the cock has come down in scrubby pines and buffaloberries on the far side of an overgrown barbed-wire fence. End of the public ground? We must have used up most of its one-mile length, but there is no sign, no livestock, no cultivation. With cold blood I would turn back anyhow, but this is the last dragon in the world and Huck is on its spoor for the third time. As I swing my legs over the fence, he trails for perhaps a hundred yards and points, head high. I circle in front to cut off the escape route. Before I get far, Huck breaks again, running now in long bounds. In the middle of one of them he turns in midair and lands on point, body twisted. His tail is high, backhairs bristling, eyes shooting fire. Bird close. Right here, boss.

I run to the far side of the trees, trying again to cut off the escape route. The cock flushes wild. Crossing shot, a little too far. Rear trigger. The pheasant comes down with its head up—meaning that it will almost certainly run. Huck appears instantly, having followed the flight line through the trees. He finds where the winged bird crashed, trails it for thirty yards, and pounces on it.

The pup fetches, but not as promptly as he would bring me a mere boot. I watch benignly as he does the pheasant strut. He has a right to show off. The bird would have run out of bounds if he had not moved fast, would have flushed out of range if he had not pointed, would have escaped if he had not caught it. It was a Huckleberry production.

The Bobwhite's Code

American hunters have a complaint that I have heard in no other country. They object to the best of the pheasant: to its energy, speed, and resourcefulness, to the way it makes a dog use his brains. The core problem is that the bird left its myth behind when it came to America. Without myth there is no satisfaction, no guidance as to what we should expect, no set of rules to make the game worth playing. Without myth we are like children being driven to Yellowstone Park: We have to ask whether we are having fun yet.

When the first Americans hiked over from Siberia, they found herds of large animals that knew no fear of man. And when another wave of immigrants came from the opposite direction some ten-thousand years later, they found game birds with no knowledge of European dogs and nets. Heath hens sat readily for a point till they became extinct. Ruffed grouse would not become serious game till the end of the nineteenth century.[1] Our rules for pointers evolved largely around one species: the bobwhite quail. To understand American bird-hunting attitudes, you must understand the eastern bobwhites of the late eighteenth and nineteenth centuries—the bobwhites that used to live from New Hampshire to Louisiana, with fewer gaps than there are today.

Behavior:

- They formed coveys, meaning that all of the birds in an area were typically concentrated in one small part of it. (This part of their behavior has not changed.)
- They were innocent. When found by a dog, they were inclined to hide rather than run or flush wild.
- They would often hold for a decisive point till the human got close enough for a shot.

Response:

- Develop a fast dog, able to search a wide area for the covey.
- Encourage bold, decisive points rather than cautious, creeping dog work, which wasted time and was less effective in holding the birds.

- To balance these traits, insist that the dog remain on point till released, even if the covey ran away. Absolute staunchness allowed the handler to regain control of a fast, bold dog before trying to relocate the covey.
- Train the dog to be "steady to wing and shot"—to hold his point even after the birds flushed and were shot or missed. This gave the gunner a chance to reload and try for the stragglers often present with covey birds.

It was splendid sport. (Still is, if you can find wild quail that will play the game.) And it was well adapted to the pointing dog's talents. Some of those were amplified in the breeding, then tested in field trials, starting in the 1870s. Bobwhites made the rules, and the rules made the dogs, and the dogs made the trainers, and by now the game is bigger than any of them. The trials are a sport in themselves—more distinctively American than baseball.

For a long time now, pen-raised bobwhites have (of necessity) been used for most of the trials. Such birds are far different from wild ones: too easy to be real game. That does not, in itself, diminish the contests, which are between dog and dog, man and man—not between man and nature. Both dogs and handlers are very good at what they do. They need a set of strict rules to make the game worth playing and the winners easier to pick. The rules have transcended their practical origin, becoming formal and stylized: a myth. I use that term here, as throughout the book, in the most respectful sense.

The Ruffed Grouse's Code

The problem is that dogs bred for such trials may not be comfortable for hunting real birds (even bobwhites) on foot. The traditional American trial emphasizes extreme range and speed at the expense of easy handling, dramatic "slam points" at the expense of caution, and staunchness on point at the expense of retrieving ability. William Harnden Foster already believed that "the more or less professional field trial game in the south . . . has developed into dog races . . ."[2] Foster's bird was the ruffed grouse, which (unlike the bobwhite) could never be hunted on horseback.

Foster and other ruffed-grouse hunters became, as best I can make out, the first group to challenge the old precepts. He used English pointers that were much faster than old American dogs, but (presumably) cautious. The Eastern grouse seldom consents to be "held", strictly speaking. A dog can at best let his human partner know of the bird's presence in time to be prepared for a shot. Some specialized dogs creep along the scent-trail for very long distances before pointing. Mind you, "creeping" does not sound elegant, so we use euphemisms. My favorite is "walking on eggs"—the dog's apparent behavior while working cautiously into a point.

So far, then, the grouse dog and field-trial bobwhite dog are quite different. They often look different, too, though both may be pedigreed English setters. This much the two mythic American game birds do have in common: Their dogs are traditionally staunch once the point is established. A dog that breaks point is likely to flush the grouse—though a few of the most cautious pointers get away with it. Most seem to creep into the point but not out of it.

Unfortunately, grouse are difficult to pen-raise and tame when one succeeds. Even so-called "grouse trials" often substitute bobwhites. I have never seen a trial with real grouse, and till I lived overseas I assumed that the old bobwhite rules were Commandments, comforting truths in an unsettled world. Staunchness was goodness and creeping was creepy.

Other Countries' Dogs

The world was in worse shape than I had imagined. Nobody else had heard of the American rules. In Brazil, Claudio Noschese and I hunted tinamous that behaved much like pheasants. His English pointers handled the birds very well: creeping, breaking point when the birds ran out, making no attempt to be steady to wing or shot. In West Africa, one good setter handled francolins in much the same way, till it overheated. In Ireland, I learned to hunt pheasants just as Huckleberry and I now do it in America—by pheasant rules, not bobwhite rules.

Portugal made a deep impression. Dogs there were carefully trained, but the rules had evolved with the red-legged partridges. Once as innocent as nineteenth-century bobwhites,[3] the partridge coveys today seldom hold for any dog's point. Portuguese trials therefore reward pointers bred to be responsive ("biddable"), cautious, and close-working—closer-working even than American grouse dogs, and vastly different from our wide-ranging, hard-to-control, slam-pointing bobwhite pointers.

I did not care for the Portuguese rules. They reduced pointing dogs to the range of flushers. It is important to be clear about the nature of my reservation, however. You will often hear pointing-dog people say that you might as well get a spaniel if you plan to keep it close anyhow. Not so. A close-working pointer still has one major advantage: He holds the bird till you are in position. You get close shots for which you are prepared.

No, the problems are different. First, a close-worker is not going to find as many birds as one that ranges far to the side. And second, a dog that potters around at close range is not as exciting to watch. That is a big thing for me. But I must report that the Portuguese were not impressed by the way I handled Trooper. He was very much an American field-trial dog despite being registered as a German shorthaired pointer.

By now it had dawned on me that rules for dogs had something to do with the birds they were supposed to hunt. The brown trout demanded respect for its old-world myth; why not a code for the bird we imported at the same time?

A Modern
Pheasant Code [4]

Teamwork

It takes a dog and a human (or two humans, but not more).

Dog scents bird. Sometimes it sits tight; cocks do so more often than most hunters are aware. The typical cock, however, tries to steal away. What happens next depends on wind direction.

Ideally, you are hunting into the wind (upwind). Your dog then strikes air-scent and follows it head-high to a point, if you are lucky, or a wild flush if you are not.

But you cannot always hunt in one direction. Even if you start with the wind right, pheasants are (I think) clever enough to run downwind when they have a choice. In this case, the dog hits only the scent that the bird has left on the ground. Such scent is weak and difficult to decipher, so the pointer may choose to run a broad loop instead—downwind without scent and then back upwind, seeking air scent. The pheasant may then be caught in the middle. But this is a risky operation, a way to manage a bad situation. If the wind is right to begin with, the dog should not try to run a loop, thereby trading good scent for bad and perhaps flushing the bird by mistake.

Expect, therefore, to give your dog active support. Keep up as best you can while he trails, helping to herd the pheasant in the right direction or head it off, as tactics demand. Two hunters can flank the dog on either side, some twenty yards out. It sounds easy. In practice it seems to be the hardest thing for new pheasant hunters to learn. Those accustomed to easier birds stroll up from behind the dog. Others just wait for something to happen, indecisively. A few see the point and freeze up more tightly than the pheasant. They get the excitement, but not the bird. A hunter who really knows how to help his dog seems almost (but not quite) as rare as a dog who really knows how to trail a pheasant.

Breaking Point

Trailing (following the scent) is by far the most difficult and important task for a pheasant dog—and the traditional American bobwhite rules discourage the pup from doing it, or learning how to do it. He must learn to use both air- and ground-scent. He must ignore rabbits and other distractions. He must stay with a bird that runs and stops, runs and stops, runs and flies. To do this he must point and follow, point and follow, point and hold. He must have enough brains to do it without command, because you will not know when to give the command.

Field-trialers and most trainers disagree. They recommend that you come up to your dog and release him from every point. It is good advice, for their game: pen-raised birds and some wild quail. Even pen-raised pheasants seldom run enough to require long trailing. But wild cocks commonly run two or three hundred yards. They do it fast, but with twists and turns and brief pauses to see whether the dog is still on the trail. A dog that loses time is very likely to lose the trail.

If you are with your dog, moreover, you are in precisely the wrong place to handle a *wild* pheasant. You ought to be many yards out, looping in from the front or side, cooperating to pin the bird. That was point 1 of the pheasant code.

Then how about a whistle release? Better, but not good. If the dog waits for your release, you may be looking for a bird that has run out and is getting farther away by the second. You cannot know that. You are nose-blind. The dog *knows*. He will learn to point the bird when it is willing to sit and otherwise trail it. Keep up with him.

A cock being trailed will often flush unexpectedly without canine misbehavior. Go ahead and shoot that bird. It is a big, hard-to-get prize, worth a high-risk, high-gain strategy.

Creeping

High-style slam-points work better on pheasants than on any other wild bird I know. A dog that makes them can hold some cocks in the strict sense of the term, and also give his owner good dreams. No dog, however, can locate wild pheasants with enough precision to slam-point every time. Caution is a function of intelligence, and a dog that has it is preferable to one that rushes in and flushes birds out of range. For me, a dog "walking on eggs" into a point also provides breathless suspense, provided that he is careful when appropriate and not simply because he is too timid to close the deal.

The Flush

The bird flushing will often be an illegal hen, and you do not want the dog to chase her far enough to disrupt the hunt. You might therefore wish to train him to be "steady to flush": staunch even when the bird flies. This also helps to control a pup that tends to be volatile, like so many Americans pointers.

I prefer to see Huckleberry run just far enough to get around visual obstacles and watch the bird. If it is a hen, or if I have missed a shot, I want him to stop. Sometimes he does. Sometimes he chases too far. We shall see whether I have placed too much faith in his ability to learn. The quick break does put him in the best position for the next step. I fancy, too, that a dog that breaks to flush is likely to retain more enthusiasm for what follows.

Trailing and Retrieving

The dog should, in any case, break at the shot, getting to the downed bird instantly. You will hear that a dog marks falls better when standing still—but the problem with pheasants is not marking. It is trailing. A pheasant is usually easy to find, if it lands dead. A running cock may be very elusive indeed, and every second's delay makes the finding more difficult.

The Risks

Few hunters of my acquaintance make their dogs steady to wing and shot (staunch through all the excitement of flushing and shooting). You may wish to do so, however, if you specialize in covey birds. In that case, it might be wise to keep the pup away from pheasants at first. They will certainly not make the training easier.

There are other risks. Listen to the professionals: If you permit the dog to make his own decisions, he will become "bad-mannered" and "untrustworthy." Those are value-loaded terms, suggestions that breaking a point is like breaking into the cash-box. Even when you subtract the adjectival excess, however, you are left with a warning that your dog—if allowed to use his own judgment—may start flushing birds on purpose.

It does not work quite that way, in my experience. The right dog points because, as we shall see in the next chapter, he carries many centuries of genetic programming. He points because he is encouraged to do so in training sessions. And he points because he learns that it is the best way to get birds for his team. He wants to do that. Huckleberry has pointed partridges and quail for twenty minutes, which is as long as it ever took me to get to him. Just this week he trailed an end-of-season cock pheasant through a broad stream-bottom, around a field of stubble, and into a grassy draw where the bird felt secure enough to hold. I crashed through the willows and got to the dog ten minutes later, in time for an easier shot than December usually offers.

You have to focus on the differences between what trainers (at least in America) call "busting" and "bumping." A dog busts birds when he tries to catch them himself instead of pointing. Pups are

especially tempted to bust pheasants that creep away from a point.
When that happens, refrain from shooting, if you have enough
moral fiber. (I'm not claiming that I do.) A dog that repeatedly
flushes birds in good, early-season cover may indeed be busting
them. It is a serious problem.

Late season is different. The ground-cover may be thin and the
birds will usually be wary. They may flush wild no matter what any
man or dog does. The best of pointers will *bump* such pheasants—
which is to say that he will flush them unintentionally. Perhaps he is
pushing them too hard, but then running pheasants must be pushed
hard if they are ever to hold. I would prefer a dog that pushes his
luck to one that creeps along on endless chases. At least the hard-
driver saves time. You are playing the odds, looking for the one cock
that wants to hide and finds a good place to do so. You and the dog
are like wolves running a band of caribou to see if one of them is
vulnerable. If predation were a hundred percent successful, you
would not wish to be a part of it, would you?

You can work off a pint of water per hour hunting like this. If
sweating is not your idea of fun, train more brakes into your pup.
Make him follow bobwhite rules and accept that you will get fewer
chances at pheasants. Or at least insist that he stop and wait for you
to catch up when a bird flushes.

Another problem arises when the pheasant dog switches to
other birds. Partridges run almost as readily as pheasants and, because the ground-cover is thinner, are more sensitive to pressure. A
dog that breaks point will bump some partridges at first: Bird-
handling is an acquired skill. The pup must learn how hard to push,
and when to back off. You can help only a little by correcting
obvious errors. Huck now seems able to switch from pheasant- to
partridge-mode when he hits the different smell, but he did not
figure this out till he was two years old.

The Eastern ruffed grouse also lives in thin ground cover and is
extremely shy. Think of American upland birds as a continuum, with
pheasants at one end, Eastern ruffed grouse at the other. The pheasant dog is bold (to pin runners). The Eastern grouse dog is cautious
(to prevent flying). In my experience, grouse dogs cope with young
pheasants, but not wise old cocks. At the other extreme, my old
Trooper pinned pheasants but could handle only the occasional
relaxed grouse. Huckleberry holds Western grouse but would proba-

bly push their Eastern relatives too hard. It is difficult for a dog to be good at both extremes—which is too bad, because extremes are exciting.

The birds elsewhere on the continuum have their own quirks, though the bobwhite is less demanding than either extreme. If you concentrate on one species, you will want a specialized dog. I do not. When I'm not near the bird I love, I love the bird I'm near, and so do my dogs.

There is another circumstance that requires retraining: switching a dog over to field trials from wild pheasants. A young dog may learn to play both games. A dog that has learned only hunting, however, will recognize pen-raised birds as defective. (I do not understand how he figures this out so quickly, but he does.) Then he will pick them up and bring them to you like cripples. This can be a disaster for trainers, whose dogs must be judged on their performance with tame birds. The sport that earns a living is the important one for a professional, or for an amateur who wants to compete with a professional.

On the other hand, a dog trained on tame birds can be at least as poor on wild pheasants, and much more difficult to retrain— perhaps impossible, after a certain age. So you have a choice to make.

Man or Nature?

There is a philosopical question too: Do you want the rules to be written by man or nature? The history of fly-fishing is a story of repeated attempts by humans to write their own rules. What always happens next is that nature, in the form of a brown trout, calls us to account. The fly must look right to the trout, not the human. I love trout. They are wild and painfully honest. They are nature. So are pheasants. If they are important to you, follow nature, and let no one tell you that her rules are inferior to those that we humans made up.

You can spend years trying to fit pheasants to inappropriate rules, learning the hard way, and, when you finally have it right, being told by every expert that you are out of line. In the end, though, many hunters must have chased pheasants in the way I have described. In that sense this pheasant code is not intended to be original.

It is not intended to be revolutionary, either. The rules here are twenty-first-century American Gothic. They are for dogs that know the meaning of "no," "come," "heel," "fetch," and "whoa." Especially whoa. For me, at least, they should not be "versatile" in the sense of chasing furry things. They should allow clean kills over solid points. They should be eager, good to watch, and smart enough to hunt a very tough bird.

Real pheasants are not impressed by human convention. They are impressed by wit and gun, legs that dance through cover and predator stare,

> O brightening glance,
> How can we know the dancer from the dance?[5]

11

✦

A Pointer
of the Veronese
School

*. . . this separation of past, present, and future is only an illusion,
however tenacious.*

Albert Einstein[1]

Your wife ought to look like Mom and your dog ought to look like Rover. You knew that when you were very young, but you did not know that you knew it. You had a dog of the mind, conscious or unconscious, functional or emotional—unless you were utterly deprived of Rovers, which is unlikely. Man's best friend may be man's only understated cliché. The dog is man's only friend, if friendship means anything. Your dog sees you as leader of his pack, not just the biped who brings food.

We have been creating the dog in our image for at least ten thousand years and possibly twice that: longer than any other animal. We started, moreover, with another species that had evolved as a member of a cooperative hunting band, not one that stalked alone like the fox or cat. You may want to think that your dog is hunting pheasants for you. He thinks that he is hunting them with you. He does not reason well, but he perceives what you want before you understand it yourself. He also runs beyond your aspirations, and he knows something at which you can only guess: where the bird is. You and dog mesh. You are strong in what he lacks, weak where he is strong. No other team has so little redundancy of skill, such economy of baggage.

The shared part adds no weight. You and your dog have the same emotions in the field. It feels odd to share things like that; uncomfortable, even, if you believe that only one of you has a soul. It happens only with man-dog working teams, and with hunters it happens in the last Edens. I would not care for Eden without a dog. I am wary of nonworking dogs, too. Some may be good. Mine were psychos, winners of a beauty contest for freaks.

Perhaps that made you angry. If it did not, something else in this chapter will do so. Anything that damages your dog of the mind cuts deep, and I am out to demolish it. I owe it to you to confess any bias. My passion for pointing dogs is already explicit, but it is not focused on any breed. All breeds are miserable.

Let me dilute that point while it is still echoing off the cliffs of your outrage. I have worn out boots behind each of this country's four major pointing breeds: English pointers, English setters, German shorthaired pointers, and Brittany spaniels. A few of each have been good. It has been the same with people: a few friends in every new place, surrounded by masses from which to escape. I am not a revolutionary seeking to abolish the whole concept of dog breeds. As an organizing principle, however, it has been so trivialized that it is just a little better than none at all.

Between you and a real pheasant dog is a long path full of pitfalls. The deepest of them is the temptation to pick a pup just because it is cute, counting on your love to make it good. The next-worst trap is breedism. There is a lot of Huckleberry in this book because he is the dog who takes me hunting, not because he is a breed.

The Outside
of the Dog

Dogs work their bodies harder than people, so dogs' bodies must be sound. Only one principle works: form follows function. Anything else, by now, looks ugly. It is a matter of culture shock. I started looking at cars in the 1950s, which was their baroque period. A nation that had once made beautiful vehicles started making them with chrome jowls, droopy eyes, atrophied muscles, short legs, and decorative excrescences. I bought a used Jaguar XK-120 coupe. It was a hawk among barnyard fowl, a protest against corruption. It was what my dog has to be now that I would rather walk than ride.

There is one other model: not my original dog of the mind but a discovery that is recent, for me. It is in a book by William Arkwright, who in turn found it in the Louvre. "The model," he says, "was evidently of high quality . . . : observe . . . the beautiful profile of the skull."[2] The drawing is reproduced in the background at the head of the chapter, lines retraced to allow clear reproduction of a pencil sketch rubbed by the centuries.

The artist who drew my model dog was Vittore Pisano, called Pisanello, of the Veronese school. His is the first known image of a pointer. It lived before English pointers or setters, before the first covey of bobwhites was ground-sluiced by a musket, before the first ruffed grouse was knocked from a limb by a pilgrim's stick. Pisanello died in 1446, forty-six years before Columbus sailed off to look for India in the wrong ocean.

What we know as the gun dog, then, came before the gun—one of those accidents that bend events in unforeseeable directions.[3] We gunners might never have had the discipline to develop the dog we needed. The original pointer's mission was to find birds, first, and then herd them into a net or hold them while the fowlers did their part. Imagine two men unfurling a long net and dragging it, afoot or by horse, over pointer and birds alike.[4] It was the ultimate test of staunchness. It required a dog of opposing characteristics: drive and discipline, eagerness and steadiness. Human campaigners with that kind of talent become generals.

Some men of wealth owned fowling dogs. "It is a matter of record," says Foster, "that Lafayette brought to this country several Spanish pointers for his personal use, although we have hard work understanding how he may have used them, since at that time wing-shooting was not practiced."[5] The explanation is to be found in the first book on American game, written in 1783. "Netting," said the author, "is entertaining, and requires excellent dogs."[6]

Most fowlers, nevertheless, must have been professional; there was a market to serve. The pointer would have been their business partner, standing between them and hunger. Fowling dogs developed in several European countries and took on different shapes. Have a look, however, at the Italian model that impressed Pisanello and Arkwright. It had small ears set high on the skull, the better to avoid snagging on thorns. It had a pronounced brow ridge, or stop, to protect the eyes. It had small jowls, one effect of which you can see in skin that is snug around the eye, protecting it from foreign matter. (Heavy jowls pull the skin down and leave a pink corner which serves as a scoop for seeds and twigs.) The tight jowls meant, too, that this dog would waste little moisture in drool.

Pisanello's model was visibly light-boned, probably small. The rest of the body must be guessed from its function and from other old Italian pictures. While I am guessing, I will assign a gender, because the dog of my dreams needs that. She would have been capable of walking miles to the fields, hunting all day, walking home, and going out again the next day. For this she would have needed a capacious chest, level back, long legs, and a long spine (relative to her weight). She would have had high-toed feet for a springy step.[7] She would have been the kind of dog that was, on the one hand, shapely enough for Pisanello, and on the other what my Portuguese friends call "rustic": tough of constitution and able to thrive on table scraps. She was (as far as I know) of no breed whatsoever.

I suspect that we have not improved on the Veronese model in five or six centuries. A great deal of the fussing over breeds has to do only with their upholstery—and Pisanello's model already had the right coat (short for heat dissipation, flat to shed burrs, and white for visibility). The history of dog-breeding is a story of crisscrossing ancient strains for nonfunctional decorations and personal whim. Even chauvinism.

In the late nineteenth century, the Germans set out to create a dog of their own as good as what the English had, but distinctively different. It would have been logical to start with the English pointer and modify it for different needs: logical, but not nationalistic. The English dog had the beautiful Veronese head so the Germans started with an ugly one, though of course they did not describe it that way.

The English pointer had short, tapered ears so the German pointer's were to be long and rounded: the worst shape. Form (and bad form at that) took priority over function. The experiment did not go well. In time, breeders emphasizing function took over.[8] Outside blood—including English—was added to the original strains and tested with German rigor in every generation. The gene pool, I imagine, was the same available elsewhere in Europe, so the best-functioning genes surfaced. The wheel was successfully reinvented.

My best friend is (according to papers that he cannot read) a German shorthaired pointer. That's if you want to be modern. My conceit is that he is an Original Veronese Fowling Dog. For a time, when he was a year old, his head could have been distinguished only by its color from Pisanello's model. He has been here before, as my wife says.

None of this is meant to suggest that the right form guarantees good work in the field. Form is merely the external equipment to do the job with a minimum of physical problems—a negative virtue. The positive virtue is function. It would not flow from form even if we humans could be trusted to pick the right one. We cannot. To call dog shows "beauty contests" is unintentional flattery. Human beauty contests at least select winners who are sound of body. Their judge is informed by natural hormones. In dog shows, on the contrary, the standards are abstract, unguided by nature. Beauty lies in the eyes of the beholder. There were beholders who thought that the 1956 Cadillac was beautiful, too.

Look at the show-strain Irish and English setters. They have everything wrong that man can breed into a dog. In the field they are flat-footed, hip-crippled, stiff-backed, short-winded, overheated, ear-torn, eye-infected, and drooly-jowled. They are as hapless as the trout produced by fish hatcheries. We designed both that way.

The Functions

Dogs with weak skills must be weeded out in every generation. In Pisanello's time, the market might have made the selection: A dog that failed to make a living for the boss would not have been bred. Today, economics do not work. Most people looking for purebred dogs play trivial pursuit. They buy a paint job, an image, or long silky hair like Mom's—anything but function. The real tests are competitive trials and hunting, with different limitations.

Hunting is the most relevant test. The problem is bias. Of ten people watching a dog in the field, nine will conclude that its talents are modest and the tenth, who happens to be the owner, will be convinced that he has a gem. He will, furthermore, tell you that he had a great pheasant season last year. He is right, if he enjoyed it. Pheasants can be hunted in more different ways than any other bird, and Rover's human has found one that both participants can handle. A human who can be objective about his best friend is either very experienced or a cold fish. Don't believe any of us.

Field trials are objective. They tell you not only which dogs find and retrieve birds, but which do it better than other dogs. It takes competition to do that. I prefer the products of competition, but many American hunters are radically dissatisfied with dogs of field-trial stock. One of the complaints is well known: Our traditional trials select for wide-running dogs. With the right rules, this problem is manageable. The complaints have led to important circuits of shoot-to-retrieve trials for unmounted hunters.

There are, however, other problems that have not (as far as I know) been widely discussed.

Some hunters are unhappy even with the products of foot-hunting trials. In any open competition among the big-four breeds, the winners are fast and energetic. They have had training to channel their energies. They have had experienced handlers. And they have been followed by humans who could do a bit of moving too, at least for half an hour within a confined area. You might prefer a dog from one of the less-popular breeds or strains—one whose line has been put through rigorous, relevant, independently judged hunting tests rather than open competitions. The problem with such breeds is their persistent "miracle-breed" advertising. You might be led to believe that your pup will find birds in unheard-of numbers. He is unlikely to be competitive, let alone miraculous, but he may be easier to follow around than a miracle.

There is another problem built into conventional trials and even some hunting tests. When professional trainers speak of "advanced work" and "a fully broken dog," they are likely to be describing *human* skills useful for trials, not *dog* skills useful for hunting pheasants. A good trainer made young Trooper steady to wing and shot. To this end, he was not allowed to retrieve till more than a year old—thereby reducing his natural wish to break point and chase a flushing bird. What happened?

- The human demonstrated skill at training.
- The dog was persuaded to obey (broken).
- The dog became a field-trial winner, a poor trailer, and a hard-mouthed retriever. I was relieved when his teeth wore down till he could only squeeze pheasants.

A real pheasant dog's functions must flow from the game described in the last chapter.

The Basics

Nose. Energy. Enthusiasm for birds. You can usually equip the pup with these qualities by choosing his parents. (It is more than you were able to do for yourself, and look how well you turned out.) Never mind distinguished ancestors farther back. Aristocracy is an appealing idea that seldom works for many generations.

Intensity

This is the trait of a bold dog that "pins" pheasants.

Hunters describe birds as pinned if they hide instead of running or flying. It is a behavior that we humans are not much good at inducing. I take a bobwhite from my recall pen (to which it will return unharmed when the training is over) and plant the bird in the grass. It runs off with its head up, watching me. Then my dog appears and the bobwhite instantly freezes, head down. It knows an effective predator when it sees one.

Wild pheasants are tougher to bluff. I know of two ways in which a dog can demonstrate the necessary intensity. One of them has not (so far as I know) been described in print.

I saw it first on November 17, 1976—the beginning pheasant season for both Bill Horn and Trooper. The three of us were in a Pennsylvania covert that was hidden from the rest of the world, back then, tucked between ramshackle farms where a nameless creek ran down to the Conococheague. No road came near. Honeysuckle climbed gray rail fences that divided fertile cornfields from rocky bottomlands. Down there a few abandoned fields were sprouting junipers. The slopes had tall hickories and tulip poplars. Gray squirrels scratched in dead leaves and the white tails of deer flickered off through a pine border. The young dog wanted to chase everything. Bill and I kept him to pheasants and bobwhites.

My diary reports that Trooper was "serving birds up on a silver platter," which was not very original but showed how good we felt. Bill had shot his first pheasant ever, and I had shot two, all over firm points. There was also a bobwhite that Trooper had pointed twice: once before I shot it, and again when it fell into the crotch of a young oak.

"Trooper got birdy again at once," the diary says, meaning that his body tensed as he followed hot scent. The trail was too long to be a quail's. It led out of the woods and into tall, dried grass where sun hit a south slope. Bill and I spread out and kept up. The dog pointed momentarily twice where the pheasant had paused, then ran on, his excitement mounting with ours. Then Trooper did the thing: *bit the ground* at a spot where the bird must have left heavy body-scent. The dog looked down, surprised to find nothing but grass in his teeth, crept another few yards, and pointed.

I moved in to flush the bird toward my friend. Nothing flushed. Trooper leaned forward, eyes bulging and spine-hair bristling, but his feet moved not an inch. Bill leaned at the same angle, same look in his eyes, gun half-mounted. Still nothing happened. I looked down. Under a thin pile of twigs, the tips of a cock pheasant's two tail feathers were barely visible. I did not know what to do next. I was pointing too, suspended between desire and inhibition. The low sun paused in its orbit for two men, a dog, and a mystery.

"Get ready," I croaked. (It is only in made-up dramas that people say useful things.) "I see it. Cock." And then I calculated where the bird's body would be from the position of its tail, reached into the brush with my hand, and grabbed. There was no more silence for some time after that. I pulled out a big bird flapping so hard that it seemed likely to lift me off the ground. Trooper jumped in to help. I held the pheasant high with my right hand to keep it from the dog's jaws. The gun was in my left hand. I could do nothing with the bird till I had both hands free. I could not bend over to put the gun down without putting the rooster within Trooper's reach. And so I stood there like a Statue of Liberty holding a torch flaming with pheasant colors.

Bill and I managed, in time, to decide (against the weight of evidence) that something was indeed wrong with the pheasant, and then to sort out guns and dog. We put the bird out of what we supposed to be its misery. We told ourselves that it was a cripple left by some other hunter. It wasn't, though, as we found when we plucked it. It was not a stocked bird, either. This was a wild, fully feathered cock in superb condition. It had simply been unwilling to risk flight with Trooper so hard after it.

You may not want to believe it and I did not either, until it happened again in each of the next two seasons. For some foolish reason—desire to possess, perhaps—I kept on trying to grab the birds with my hand, till I flushed a cock, tried to shoot from my knees, and missed with both barrels. (Do not laugh too hard till you've tried it.) After that the toe of my boot seemed like a better pheasant-prodder.

Huckleberry first bit the grass (and then went on to point) when he was eighteen months old, a little younger than Trooper. It can happen with any running bird, but only within seconds after it has paused and moved on. I think the dog must detect what we humans call "body scent," in our imprecise way: not air scent, not ground scent, but a smell that means the bird is *right there*, though of course it is not. The dog's behavior shows how thoroughly its nose dominates its eyes. Most birds are, of course, pointed without an example of ground-biting, but I know of nothing that demonstrates intensity so irrefutably. I do not know how many dogs ever show this behavior. If the percentage is small, the test is especially useful.

The other test is easier to stage, easier to pass, and more open to subjective interpretation: watch the pup when he suddenly hits scent and points a close, wild bird. Look for shining eyes, hair bristling along the spine, quivering muscles. Look for a stiff, awkward posture, sometimes with a foot raised. The dog stays in such a position because his comfort does not matter. Only the scent counts.

The tail is part of the tableau. If the tail waves slowly, the dog is said to be "flagging"—a reliable sign of low intensity. The height of the tail matters much less, being governed by bone structure. High tails are in fashion, however. Look closely at any late-twentieth-century photograph of field-trial winners posing with their pointing dogs. You will see a detail that is going to make these images period-pieces. The proud owners are holding their dogs' tails up, by hand.

English pointers and German shorthaired pointers have many individuals that point intensely. Some English setters strains are equally intense, but they differ so widely that one needs to think of them as almost four separate breeds: show dogs, grouse dogs, field dogs, and trial dogs. The first two tend toward the personalities that hunters call "soft" (as opposed to bold, intense, or hardheaded). If you want a setter, be doubly careful in screening out unsuitable lineages, but the best are as good as anything out there.

If one were to shave the best pheasant dogs in any of the above breeds—English setters, English pointers, and German shorthaired pointers—they would be difficult to distinguish. The resemblance may not be coincidental. The English pointer was the fastest of the three, and speed won American trials, so the other two breeds began to look more and more like English pointers. Setters developed shorter coats. Some German shorthairs became white. Both acquired faster bodies. Maybe it was just willpower, a matter of dams deciding to make their pups look like that dashing English pointer stud who lived a few doors down the row of kennels. At least in the case of shorthairs, however, injections of English-pointer blood have been officially sanctioned.

The fourth main pointing breed in this country is the Brittany spaniel. It would look different even shaved, and it was developed (in France) to hunt differently. Then, in America, it was bred to compete in our trials. Brittanies now vary almost as widely as setters in range, temperament, and intensity. I have walked past individuals that I thought were taking a rest and been startled when the birds flushed. At the other extreme was Tom Eversman's Brittany, which broke a leg but kept going till it caught a wounded pheasant. Now that is intensity for you.

Do not confuse intensity with social problems. There are pointing dogs that are too aggressive (especially in some German breeds) and dogs that are too high-strung (especially among setters and spaniels), but there are also intense, stable personalities in the same breeds. Dogs from proven working-strains should be keen during the hunt and relaxed in the den. My nonhunting wife does not share my enthusiasm for English pointers, but they are not pushy in the living room—just bored. I can sympathize with that, so maybe you shouldn't trust me on a matter like intensity. Pheasants are intense. My dogs are intense. I could be a bit hard-headed myself.

Precocity

There is a tide in the affairs of pups which, taken at the flood, leads on to fortune. Omitted, all the voyage of their lives is bound in shallows and in miseries. Huckleberry's flood came when he was six months old. At seven months he was a better pheasant-hunter than Trooper after seven seasons. Maybe Huck was born with more talent, but I think he just caught the tide.

All a dog really needs to know he should learn in kindergarten. You must start with the right pup, of course. Allow me to quote another dog-training expert: "precocious pups are winners; pups displaying little or no natural ability are losers . . . we'd have better gun dogs if more sportsmen would cast a colder eye at pointing-breed pups that don't flash-point early and . . . [at] all breeds that won't naturally chase after a thrown object . . . or have to be urged to get out and quest for game. . . . Given the opportunity, good pups will be showing you something by the time they are seven or eight months of age."[9]

The flash-pointing test is easy. You tie a bird's wing or a rag on the end of a line, tie the line to an old fishing rod, and flop the wing in front of the pup. When he pounces, you whip the wing away. Don't let him catch it. He will start pointing the thing. He will probably do it when very young indeed. This is like watching one of those Japanese infants playing real Beethoven on the violin. You melt.

Many English and German shorthaired pointer strains are precocious. So are some English setters. Others take too long to settle down. Be ruthless in screening the parents, but then go ahead and take the risk. You might be tempted to bypass it by getting a dog old enough to have proved itself. This sounds logical. It is one of the two beginnings likely to produce a dog that runs off and hunts for itself (the other being a pup from a wild strain). Get yours when he is young enough to form a bond: not less than eight weeks old but not much more, either.

Then be with him when the tide rolls in.

Range

Pheasant-hunters are among those who most urgently demand close-working dogs. The case is this: Lots of cocks flush wild, either without provocation or because the dog blunders. If the dog stays close enough, his owner may get a shot anyhow. That's one way to do it, but not mine.

I want a pup with a five-speed transmission. When he hits the right smell, he should shift down and work out the trail, which may be slow business. He should have four-wheel-drive, too. If the birds are in ditches clogged with cattails, then he should push through them. But when scent is hard to find, he should shift to overdrive-fifth and look for birds in a swath ten times broader than I could cover on my own.

But of course close-working dogs have other purposes.

Size of coverts: where they are small, a fast dog is hard to handle. He'll sweep the whole thing, get bored, and go hunting for the neighbor's cat.

Visibility: most hunters (including me) prefer close-ranging dogs for woodcock and ruffed grouse, because one cannot see far in their cover.

The human factor: Huck strains my powers of telepathy. Slow down, you little brown expletive. Give me a chance to see some scenery that's not filtered through sweat. Aren't there any birds back here in my part of the farm? Oooo . . . easy . . . whoa . . . beautiful. Hold that rooster, boy. Help is on the way. Little brown dog, how I love thee.

These are the strongest sensations in adult human life. By "adult," I mean post-skirt-chasing life, because eventually you catch a woman you like, and then you ought to chase something different (especially if you are a candidate for high office). You are too young to stop vibrating between despair and reward. Maybe you will never be ready to stop, in your mind. You wouldn't have to worry about catching Huckleberry.

One of these years my body will catch me, though. I will be standing out there, breathing hard and smiling wide and holding up a fresh-slain dragon, when thump! Body will catch up with spirit as if attached to an elastic that I have been stretching thin all these years.

So I am keeping my mind and eyes open. What I hope to see is a close-working pup that can find as many birds as Huck. Even *almost* as many. Such a dog must exist; I keep hearing about him. So far, though, the best bird-finders have been the pups that wanted to follow their noses a bit too far on occasion. Which humans do you bet on for tough jobs: the nine-to-fivers or the hard-drivers?

That's the trouble with dogs. They're too much like people.

Trailing and Retrieving Ability

Pheasants run. Trooper could not trail them reliably. He had an unusually good nose (as his trials demonstrated), but he knew how to work only air-scent. He lost opportunities, at best; wounded birds at worst. To lose a wounded bird is to be responsible for a tragedy.

Trooper's problem was (I think) nurture, not nature. With

Huckleberry, we did everything the other way around. We praised him for anything he retrieved. Anything. There are times now when we would prefer that he not fetch rugs, bags of groceries with the pickles falling out, and gut-piles from somebody's deer. Of the birds I shot in his first full season, however, Huck found every one that came down where we could reach it. One flew off-limits onto property where we could not get permission to follow. To make up for that, he brought me two cocks that other hunters had shot and failed to find. He trailed one winged bird for three-quarters of a mile, several others for long distances. Off-season, he fetched live young magpies. Twice he brought me fully grown, protesting go-phers. I turned them loose undamaged. Virtue is boring, so Huckle-berry is not as much fun to read about as old Trooper. He is more fun to hunt with.

We got German shorthairs because my wife did not like English pointers. Anna can barely tell one breed from another, which makes her immune from breedism. The shorthair's Wagnerian history both-ered me until I persuaded myself that Huck was the Original Veronese Fowling Dog resurrected. He is also about the same in form and function as the old-style English pointers with which my Grand-father Carryer hunted bobwhites back in Missouri. My pup's color is worse but his trailing ability may be better.

Still, there are English pointers and setters that do learn to trail well, given a chance when they're young. More of them deserve that chance.

High Head

The business end of a howitzer is called the muzzle. A pointing-dog's nose should normally be in the same position, up high. The rest of him is just a nose-carriage. Air-scent is the only kind that can be worked at the speed you have a right to expect from a pointer. When air-scent works, a dog that can use it finds even winged pheasants much faster than a dog ground-trailing.

The problem is that air-scent soon develops gaps. They can be reliably closed only by a dog that gets his nose down near the ground. A clever high-headed pup should learn to do that. A natu-rally low-headed dog probably lacks the scenting ability or the genes to get his nose up. Give him to someone who just wants a pet.

Training

Pups need formal training, if only because the bird season is too short. A determined little devil like Huck could have used more obedience-work than I gave him. It is not the part I enjoy. Get advice from someone who is better at it—perhaps a professional. But do not think of training as a substitute for hunting. Only fields and wild birds will make your pup as clever, bold, and enthusiastic as his inheritance allows.

It gets down to the difference between training and teaching. You can train a pup to avoid behavior you do not want. If he has the right instincts, you can encourage him to intensify habits that are useful to you. You cannot teach him to hunt. You do not know the real game. We humans see cock pheasants in the air, or strutting over a field in the distance, and have to deduce the rest. Only the dog can sense every move they make. Only he knows their resourcefulness and strength, and he learns only when he has chased them through enough cornfields and cattails, weeds and woods. If he learns to hunt when hunting is hard, for days on end—finding, working, cooperating, pointing, trailing, retrieving—then he is your miracle. He is a set of genes between accidental history and degenerate future, an intersection with your orbit, a comet burning as you watch.

Part V

Armor, Gun,
and Flavor

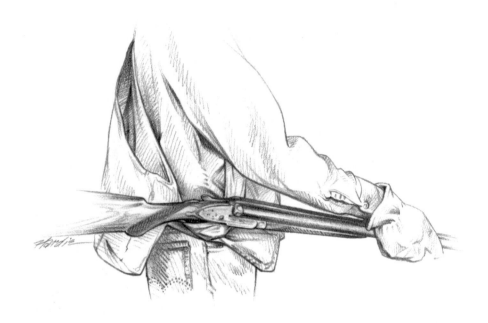

12

⤙

Armor

Out here in God's country there is a fellow who digs up bones, and he concludes (if I have this right) that dinosaurs did not go extinct: They grew feathers and turned into birds. The family has plasticity. Well, then, if pheasants are dinosaurs, we are clearly correct in dressing like St. George on November Saturdays, because everybody knows that dinosaurs and dragons are the same.

You need armor in this sport more than any other. Like the hero of Celtic myths, you enter a disturbed landscape when you follow the pheasant: disturbed not by the faerie (I think) but the farm. With trees gone and sod broken, briars and wild roses move in, and brambles and buffaloberries, hawthorns and thistles. You must wade in them as an angler wades the stream. No dog will thrash through the thorns all day if his human tiptoes through the tulips. The flightiest of dogs will be steady on point rather than enter a patch of those pretty red prickle-bushes. That is when you must keep the pledge you made to your pup: whither thou pointest, I will go.

The complication is that you must also follow your dragon a long distance. He is seven times as large as a bobwhite and (other things being equal) about seven times as scarce. During the season, you and your dog will lose weight steadily. If the season lasted all year there would come a time when your weight curves would intersect with zero and you would both enter a perfect state of nothingness: nirvana. As it is, the season is over too soon, and there is little hope of extinguishing the self in this manner.

All good recreations have creation in them. In some kinds, however, you can reinvent just your mind. Pheasants get your body involved in the excitement, whether you like it or not.

So your armor must be light as well as tough. There is an equation: $E_h - E_p = D$. Energy (hunter's) minus Energy (pheasant's) equals Dinner. Weight saps energy.

Legs

For years I broke in new jeans by hunting. They were cheap and full of character, but my legs came to look like maps of Italy with the roads etched in red, and I found myself shirking the thorns.

The solution is nylon, a fabric with no character, great strength, and a talent for drying quickly. It turns the barbs of outrageous fortune and is of help against the occasional serpent's tooth. It should run all the way up the front of your pants' legs, and part of the way up the back. Come to think of it, a strip of this armor in the crotch would inspire confidence as you teeter on a barbed-wire fence. Why don't they make the whole thing of nylon with a coarse weave? It would save the weight of a double layer.

Before you buy, produce a spring scale and weigh the pants. They should not exceed twenty-four ounces, which is less than a pair of jeans. On a warm day you would curse anything heavier. Should you need more warmth in late season, add thin long johns of a synthetic fiber that does not hold moisture. If the day is both wet and cold, wear waterproof nylon chaps on top.

Feet

Pheasant-walking is hope. That makes it nonexercise, the best kind. You slip past a barn collapsing on its timbers and a harrow rusting into the weeds. Nothing but hunting lasts. Farms hang between growth and decay, city and wilderness, more comfortable than either. Farmland is flat—as nature goes—so you can swing your feet over it with the heedless regularity of a grandfather clock's pendulum. You do not need winding often; your body evolved for this. Fields and woods flow by like running water. You and your companion want to chatter like old Izaak Walton and Venator on their seventeen-mile stroll to the Thatched-house, but talk frightens pheasants, so you hum to yourself.

That's if your feet do not hurt.

You need only one of everything else, but take two or three pairs of boots. Work out the socks that fit each pair best and take extras of those, too. Change them as the day changes.

Morning means dew in humid country, and wet grass has a strange soaking property. You may splash across streams dry-shod but the dew will get through unless you wear rubber. The British Wellington boots evolved in the right climate and are comfortable forever if worn with inner socks that wick moisture through to special, absorbent outer socks—low ones covering just the feet. Most American rubber boots are badly designed, but at least one company (La-Crosse) is making them right. Things to avoid: laces, insulation, tight toes, loose heels, tops less than sixteen inches high, and weight over three-and-three-quarter pounds for a pair of size eleven boots.

For swamps and streams, take hip boots, also light.

If the day turns warm and dry, get out of the rubber. Lightweight, old-style, American-made leather boots are the best if you can afford them. I have had good luck with Russells and Redwings, which seem to be made by people with feet like mine.

The new high-technology boots will get their design right one day. Their light weight is splendid, but those I have tried were made for people who hike once a week, on trails.

- Once-a-weekers do not seem to mind boots with sewn-in waterproofing and insulation. Hunters need waterproofing that can be renewed (as with wax) and insulation that can be removed to dry (as with socks).
- Trails get worn down to rocks, so trail boots favor lug soles. Farms run to mud (which turns lug soles into ten-pounders) and snow (which turns them into skis).
- Trail-hikers do not mind low boots. Hunters need tops well above the ankle-bone to keep out seeds, pebbles, and snakes that go bump in the grass.

What I wind up wearing over much of the season, therefore, is a pair of Bean boots: the rubber-footed, leather-topped kind. They are a triumph of experience over design. The rubber-to-leather seam leaks and rubs my heel, but I do not use the boots in serious moistness and have figured out the right combination of socks and moleskin for the rest of the time. The tops come in any height and, being leather, wear well. The soles shed mud. The bottoms are compact and light. They do not wear long, but the makers will sew on replacements for a fair price. This appeals to us tightwads.

Hands

I wear gloves even in early season, claiming that they protect my hands from thorns, but they also protect my pretty gun from sweat, which matters more. In cold weather there is no choice. You might like to know that even a man with chronically cold fingers can shoot a double-triggered gun in temperatures below zero Fahrenheit. There is a trick: Avoid "shooting gloves," which is to say, those intended for use with trigger-finger intact. They are by nature thin, tight, and cold. Leather has no insulating value.

Instead, buy any glove that fits the season—but loose, and with long cuffs. Buckskin wears well (unlike kid) and stays soft after a wetting (unlike steer). Get undyed leather, if you can find it, because those pretty browns and yellows will stain your hands and your gunstock. As the fields turn white, go from unlined to thickly insulated leather. By season's end, add a pair of thin synthetic glove-liners. These may be stretched really tight, unlike leather, and will not hinder the trigger-finger.

Now the trick: cut a short, longitudinal slit in the trigger finger of the leather gloves, starting an inch or so down from the tip. You can pull your finger inside for warmth and stick it back out again instantly, for shooting. It is hard to believe that such a simple modification could make hardware-store gloves better than the most expensive "shooting gloves"—but it does.

Head

Brightly colored hats are ugly and may frighten the occasional high-flying pheasant. Look on them, however, as a kind of extra-shiny armor, not shot-repellent but shot-preventing. One day in Maryland, a friend of mine fired into a bush where another was standing. The shooter was one of the most careful I have ever met, and he was (thank goodness) using fine shot. The other friend had gone off on his own, then returned unannounced. No one got hurt. All of us developed an interest in counter-camouflage.

Many hats today are made of waterproof plastic. Avoid them unless you intend to cook *cervelle à la chasseur*.

Visors let heat escape and do not snag on limbs. They also fit best. If your hair is thin, however, baseball-type caps prevent sunburn where it hurts. In the humid East, you may not need to worry about sunburned ears, but they give Western dermatologists the chance to perform some interesting operations. The solution is a narrow brim—not the kind that blocks your vision when you look down the barrels of a shotgun. Here is a way to be sure: Look through your shooting glasses. If the brim comes below the top of the frame, you have a problem.

The glasses are literally armor. Get shot-proof plastic for light weight.

Trunk

The designers will try to sell you coats—maybe high-technology models with waterproof membranes and zip-in liners. These may be all right for sitting in duck blinds. In the uplands, they turn hunter into self-basting turkey. They are recommended only by fashion. Definition:

Fashion is a way of getting you to buy what you do not need in order to hide what you do not want.

Instead, buy for function. Wear a long-sleeved cotton shirt, changing it to flannel as the season progresses. Still later, add a long-sleeved undershirt and an unlined nylon shell—the kind that unzips all the way down the front, for ventilation. My old shell from Mr. Bean weighs nine ounces and is just right.

Avoid pull-over garments and bulky ones that impede gun-mounting. In a pinch, dense wool shirts provide warmth without bulk, but they collect almost as many burrs as full-feathered Irish setters. Try shivering instead. Usually the wool shirt is excess baggage within the hour; and so is the shell, unless there is a wind.

If it rains, leave the shell in the car and wear instead a coat of light, *unlined* wax-proof cotton. It will let sweat pass through while keeping out most of the damp most of the time. It will do this for years, if you brush on a new coat of wax now and then.

The Bird-&-Shell-&-Gun-Pack

Over the above garments (in any combination and in any season) goes the pack. Now the first thing to remember is that the pack is not clothing, has nothing to do with clothing, and is best when it least resembles clothing. We often say "vest" because there is no short term in English for bird-&-shell-&-gun-pack. The Germans probably have a long word. The British say "waistcoat" because, well, the British wear clothing in the field. In America we are still in days of old when knights were bold, and what we want is armor.

Of all the outdoor gear that makes me cranky—and there is plenty of it—the atrocities called "shooting vests" are the worst. Eschew anything that looks like a real vest, which is to say a coat with the sleeves cut off. Such impedimenta will not keep you warm in the cold or dry in the wet, but in the heat they will simmer you and any birds that you are fortunate enough to be carrying inside the "fully lined, bloodproof game pouch."

Start the design by picturing the kind of tight-fitting rucksack worn by rock-climbers. It should be just large enough for three pheasants. The part of it next to your back should be of washable nylon cloth. The outside should be of heavy, wide-meshed netting, like that on some fishing vests. This looks fragile but is not. Most important: The game-pocket *is* the pack and not an add-on. It must not unsnap, unzip, unbutton, unfold, unpucker, or otherwise infuriate. If it is capable of these sins, it will commit them when loaded with pheasants. Count on it.

The shape of the pack is critical for the same reason. All of it must remain close to your back. There must be no pouch drooping down. Most makers give you the droops because most makers have not carried one pheasant, let alone three. (Sporting fashions are made by people who swoon at the thought of dead birds or of walking, let alone the two in combination.) When a swinging pouch is filled with pheasants, it behaves like a wrecking ball, or like the foul that is called "clipping" in football. With every stride you get a clip on the back of your legs—the rooster's revenge.

The bird-carrier differs from the climber's rucksack in that there is an opening on each side, near the top. You can insert a pheasant without taking the pack off. With a practice, you can also remove and stow your nylon shell on the run.

There should also be ammunition pockets that extend forward from the pack on each side of your waist. Inside the pockets should be shell-loops to keep ammunition from bouncing out. Avoid shell-loops that are not in pockets. Fashion-wise, they are macho, very Pancho Villa. Functionally, the wearer more closely resembles Johnny Appleseed, except that ammunition does not germinate when sprinkled in the fields. Shell loops—especially the elastic kind—spew their contents out at random as you walk. The exposed rims of shotshells also do a fair job of checkering your gunstock where you may not want it checkered.

There should be no hardware of any kind on the part of the pack that is in front of your body. Hardware scratches stocks.

Somewhere there should be a couple of outside pockets for your dog's water-bottle and a first-aid kit. The kit should include a hemostat to pull thorns and porcupine quills or, if the worst happens, to clamp the pup's artery while you carry him out on your shoulders. In Brazil we carried serum for snake bites too.

Carrying the Gun

A well-designed bird-pack can also carry a shotgun, which is an immense convenience. This may be news. I have not seen anyone else using the trick.

Hold the gun pointing straight forward on either side of your body. Then hook the trigger guard in above the shell-pocket. The shoulder straps will take the weight of the gun. This is almost as effortless as carrying your gun on a sling, but fast enough to shoot a surprise bird. You *must* keep one hand on the barrels to steady them, however, and to keep them pointing in a safe direction. A gun so carried points forward and down—at your dog or foot, if you are careless. But any gun is easy to point dangerously if carried to be shot quickly. The customary cross-body carry is less risky for your dog but more likely to threaten your partner, because the gun points sideways. My keen sense of mortality comes from getting a good look at it in the dark depths of gun barrels.

Here is how to check your new pack: Put fifteen shells in front and ten pounds of dried, bagged beans (equivalent to three pheasants and the dog's water) in the rear. Then take a fast walk with spurts of running—interval training for November. Finally, send the torture apparatus back for a refund. I bribe seamstresses to modify my nonvests, and they are still not much good. Maybe some maker will get around to trying the bean-bag test before violating your human rights with his product.

Breaking It In

If you appear with all-new armor, your friends will send you off on your own. They know the odds. The crotch of your breeches will rip from coccyx to codpiece when you swing your leg over a fence, or you will hike two miles into a dismal swamp and discover that all of your ammunition has bounced out, or you will achieve a nice red glow from breathable clothing that didn't.

The cure is field-testing, but of course you are too busy for that. Here is a way to achieve credibility—even comfort. Toss in the laundry everything that is not to be used specifically for rain (hat, chaps, and wax-proofed jacket). Be merciless with the rest. If a tag says "do not launder," all the better. Washing will add character and remove waterproofing, which provides that juicy self-basting effect.

Mind you, nylon is tough stuff. You might be forced to let your dog tenderize it as a confidence-building measure. Before sleeping on it he will scratch it into submission and chew a bit here and there. You may then venture into the field without causing the dragon to snicker.

13

✦

Getting It
Right
(t h e   G u n)

Myths have blood. You cannot grow them in the garden, decide on them at staff meetings, or create them in situation comedies. Look away if you wish, but a hunter must not. Before he can redeem the bird he must shoot it, watch colored feathers drift away, reach into the body cavity, get blood on his hands. He cannot do it without a gun. It sounds like a horrible artifact. It is a treasure, life and death. It is not even the most important piece of gear, objectively—that would be boots—but it is the one that matters.

Because guns have mattered to so many people over so many years, they are highly developed. A one-chapter treatment must assume some previous knowledge on your part. If you lack it, the writers identified in the footnotes can help. [1]

My gun was made in 1896. In 1975 I leased it for the remainder of one lifetime, which is not a long-term lease as Mr. Woodward's guns go, but I have been apologizing ever since. It happened that I was living near London when "best guns" cost less than a month's wages, so of course I got one. (If that makes sense to you, read on. Otherwise kindly skip to the next chapter.)

Where I went wrong was in hunting with the Woodward. Most people with such guns have the wit not to use them. They are left home as hunting-surrogates, objects in which to find solace when other forms of escape are not possible. Mine gets the work it was built for. I keep it perfect, though. I strip it down to dry after a rain and clean it religiously. (Note choice of adverb.) If you do not think that shotguns need to be cleaned, you should peer into the innards of as many old ones as I did while shopping. I also learned, while poking around in there, that one or two of the great old gunmakers had a flexible notion of "best." Not Mr. Woodward. He got it right.

I heard that first from the coach at a London shooting school, who worked out stock measurements as I shot clay pigeons. We need not worry about the metal parts, he said: the barrels would shoot to the same point, and they would be regulated for an even pattern. Mr. Woodward would have got them right. In Portugal, a few years later, I took the gun in for a new stock. Another customer was there ahead of me with a top-grade Perazzi, which I admired. Its breech would handle higher-pressure loads than mine. Its trigger-plate and stock were quick-removable, so that the metal parts could be dried easily. Then the gunsmith—a cranky old artist, like many of his kind—did something embarrassing. He swept Mr. Perazzi's best to a corner of the counter, put Mr. Woodward's down in the middle, and gazed with devotion. "*Esta sim é espingarda,*" he said. "Now this is a gun."

Whether by magic or science, my shooting improved. On doves and partridges, I made runs. Under pheasant-hunting conditions it would be hubris to think of runs, but at least those bang-bang-damns at the day's only cock—moments that recycle in nightmares—became less common. For the first time I had no consciousness of how much I had led the bird or where I had aimed. The gun shot itself. My only accomplishment as a shooter is that I found the gun of a lifetime while there was a fair bit of lifetime left.

Let us get one thing out of the way, however: It makes no

economic sense to spend more than the price of a pump gun—an Ithaca, perhaps, still make as it always was; or an old Winchester model 12, better-looking than most doubles. I like the toolness of the pump guns, the way they clank like 1932 Fords. I would enjoy carrying one around to aggravate the dudes. It happens, however, that I shoot better with a double-barreled gun, for reasons that will emerge. Most other upland gunners are the same. Today I could find a double costing less than the Woodward—but perhaps no less than it cost in 1975—and I would not love it as much. And hunting is irrational anyhow.

The Woodward was far from my first double-barreled shotgun, but I still have the first one too. It is an old Winchester Model 24, as close as I could afford to the recommendations of Jack O'Connor. He was a gun-writer so persuasive that "American model" guns anywhere in the world are now made to his specifications. People in Europe do not use such guns, however. They export them to us. Mr. O'Connor was a rifleman with a fine taste for practicality and style, in rifles. He used upland guns that imitated rifles, with short barrels, single triggers, beavertail fore-ends, and raised ribs. Or maybe it was Elmer Keith (a writer of almost equal influence) who wanted the ribs. On an over-under gun, these things do not look bad. On a side-by-side, they add up to the Full Cleveland. On any gun they detract from function in the field.

A Gun for Pheasants

Let us therefore back up and build a gun around the problems that the pheasant creates for us, first; and then around the problems that we manage to create for ourselves.

Pheasant Problems

1. *Range.*   In this as in so many things, pheasants go to extremes. Many fly while the hunter is barely in range. The wild flushes are, moreover, typically low and fast. (I have watched a trained falcon that could take ducks almost at will, but not pheasants behaving in this way.) At the other extreme, some cocks lie tight, hoping not to

be found, and then escape behind brush. You have to take close-range snap-shots.

A gun for both extremes needs two barrels, two very different chokes—and two triggers. The "selective" feature of single triggers is too slow and not intuitive. With two triggers, the open-choked barrel shoots itself when a bird gets up close. If it is distant, the tight barrel goes off. If you are caught with only one barrel loaded, you pull that trigger. Everybody does it, except Americans, and more of us are learning. It is about the only thing in all of shotgunning that I do right. It must not be very difficult.

By good fortune, the right barrel of my Woodward came cylinder-bored—with no choke at all. I would not have had the courage to order that on a new gun. The pattern is even, good to some thirty yards, better than anything else up close: a cure for the bang-bang-damns. The left barrel has a modified choke and puts almost twice as many pellets in the conventional thirty-inch circle at forty yards (sixty-plus percent instead of thirty-plus, with factory loads). It is good at forty yards but much too tight at twenty, where many shots offer. The modified choke is by no means the good compromise that many hunters seem to consider it.

2. *Environment.* You walk miles through grass and mud and storms, with few shots. Your gun should be foolproof and no more than seven pounds in weight. Pump guns are reliable, and a few are light, but of course none offer an instant choice of chokes. Over-and-under guns work very well, though you will not find many on the market with double triggers. Side-by-side guns are the lightest and most compact of all. They are very unlikely to let you down in the field if you avoid single triggers (which are subject to a remarkable range of ailments). The problem with side-by-sides is that they peaked too soon. Most are still made to the 1875 Anson and Deeley box-lock design, and there have been no major improvements since about 1890. There is no room for improvement in quality or function; the best of the old guns came as close to perfection anything made by man ought to come. Unfortunately, their design required expensive labor. Over-and-under designs have had more recent attention, and they cost less for the same quality. Strange how often simplicity comes at a premium.

3. *Clean kills.* Not easy, with a cock pheasant. Our traditional "maximum loads" have too much recoil for a light gun, and they often dissipate their energy in a poor shot-pattern. I hand-load hard shot in size 7, occasionally 6. (It happens to be Italian nickel-plated shot, but premium copper-plated shot may be as good.) This stuff gives the penetration of larger shot, though not the energy, and it puts enough pellets in the load to provide respectable density even with my open-choked barrel. My heavy load is 1⅛ ounces at 1200 feet per second. Mostly I use 1¹⁄₁₆ ounces, the load with which Mr. Woodward patterned the gun in 1896.

4. *Hitting with a light gun.* Balance helps. Look on it as a way to make a gun carry light and shoot heavy. This will take some explaining, so there is a separate section on the subject at the end of the chapter.

5. *Rising birds.* A rooster may go almost straight up, especially if he is caught between you and an obstacle, and even pheasants that seem to be flying level will usually be rising slightly. Raise the comb of your stock (with a moleskin pad, if necessary) until your pattern centers about six inches over the point of aim at forty yards. This is good for crossing shots too. Instead of swinging your muzzle through the target, blotting it out, you can swing through the bottom edge.

Human Problems

1. *Shooting left.* At skeet, or a patterning board, this problem may not be noticeable. You have time to place your feet carefully, lining your right eye up with the rib. In the field, however, the pattern may tend to go off-center—especially if you have raised the comb, or if your joints are a bit stiffer than they used to be when you were on the baseball team. Consider cast-off. It is a slight bend to the right of the stock. It is usually almost imperceptible, but it gets the right eye in the right place.

2. *Flinching.* The best solution is to be twenty-two years old and well-padded between the ears. Otherwise:

   a. Avoid heavy loads with an upland gun.

b. Get a recoil pad. It is one doodad that works, and you can at last buy good American pads without decoration.

c. Check the trigger pulls. You may not notice them, on a shotgun, but if they get too heavy, you flinch and miss. The Woodward's front trigger has a pull of 3½ pounds; the rear (which must be a little heavier to give the same feel) fires at 4 pounds. Both are crisp. I do not think that anyone has touched the sears since 1896.

3. *Safety.*   We are all careful. Now—please raise your hand if you have never found your gun pointing in a direction that frightened you, or noticed your partner's gun pointing at you. There do not seem to be many hands waving out there. You might like to ponder the fact that the safety mechanism of most guns blocks only the trigger, not the hammers. It is possible to make a safety that blocks hammers too. The Woodward has one, and it works. Such a safety could be designed into most guns at slight extra cost, if enough of us were to insist on it. Mind you, it is not needed often. Maybe just once in a lifetime.

Balance

Balance, as a metaphor, is synonymous with good. It is desired by everybody, or at least by everybody who can afford an expensive shotgun. Anglers used to weight their fly reels just to achieve balance—though it made casting more difficult. Let me make clear, therefore, that this is about balance not as a way of life but as a physical attribute of guns. In light game-guns, the right balance helps. It costs something but expensive guns do not always have it.

Back to first principles. A balance, in its original sense, is a weighing device. It has a swinging beam with a pan for weights at each end. In guns, by extension, balance has to do with the distribution of weight between the extremities.

The best balance for a game gun is different from that for a target gun, which may be why the concept has remained fuzzy. At skeet I shoot best (which is not saying much) with a nine-and-one-half-pound autoloader that has about the balance of a truck axle. For the uplands, that gun is much too heavy to carry and too slow to mount. The trick is to come up with one that is light when I carry and mount it, but precise when I shoot it. That really is a trick—a way to fool my reflexes.

One British writer and engineer, Gough Thomas,[2] had the courage to measure balance. I shall start by borrowing the two qualities he chose.

1. *Low moment of inertia.*   A gun has this if its weight is concentrated between the shooter's hands. Such a gun is fast-handling—quicker to swing than one with the same weight spread out over a greater distance. Mr. Thomas measured moments of inertia and found that double-barreled guns came out best; their compact actions keep much of the gun's weight between the hands.

My opinion, now: Gough Thomas was measuring something that is useful in a gun, but only up to a point. If weight concentration were an absolute good, we could improve any gun's balance by cutting back its barrels and using lighter material for the stock. Many old writers insisted on short barrels for the uplands, and many of us tried them. I found them about as effective as rock-throwing. Come to think of it, a good throwing rock has a low moment of inertia.

I think the problem, conceptually, is that weight concentration is not really balance. Picture the old balance beam. Now take an equal amount of weight from each extremity and move it to the middle. The beam will become faster-swinging and less stable—but when it settles, its pointer will be in the same place.

2. *Point of balance about half-way between the hands (when the gun is held in shooting position).*   This is Mr. Thomas's second quality. Find it by resting the gun on a finger and noting the point at which it balances. Then hold the gun with your hands in their normal shooting position and note whether the point of balance is closer to the front hand (muzzle heavy), closer to rear (muzzle light), or in the middle. Repeaters, because of their long receivers, tend to have more weight forward.

This test measures real fore-and-aft balance and is important. Thomas's explanation: "When one attempts to change the direction of a gun by a relative movement of the hands, it tends to turn about the least moment of inertia; and it is clearly desirable that the point about which the gun *tends* to turn should be the same as that about which one is trying to *make* it turn."

There is a problem that Thomas did not mention: The gun turns about a different point as soon as it is mounted. Think of an old-fashioned set of scales with a beam four feet long, weighing seven pounds. To pick the beam up comfortably, you would put your hands at equal distances from its center. Next, however, transform the beam to a gun and mount it. In that position, the gun no longer turns about its own center. The pivot becomes (approximately) your spine; you swing your whole body to shoot. The easiest gun to swing then will be one that has more than half of its weight near the body. Experience bears this out. Here is Bob Brister's conclusion: "A gun balanced muzzle-light will swing and handle better for hunting. But clay-target scores will be higher with a muzzle-heavy balance. The difference basically is that clay targets continue their original direction but birds do not necessarily fly that way."[3]

This leads to a practical recommendation. A beavertail fore-end adds weight in a bad place for a game gun, out in front of the triggers. Such a fore-end can make a double-barreled gun feel like a repeater. The weight is unnecessary. Most of it comes from excess baggage—wood as broad as a beaver all the way to the rear of the fore-end, where you should not hold the gun. If you have a side-by-side double, try this: find the right position for your left hand and leave a thin layer of wood rising partway up the barrels there. Then taper back to the profile of a splinter fore-end at the rear. Such a fore-end (done right) has none of the disadvantages of most compromises. It looks even better than the traditional splinter and gives a grip more comfortable than a beaver's bottom.

The pistol grip adds only a little weight, and that in a better place. My pet gun has a grip of unusual shape that I have retained in honor of Mr. Woodward. Unlike some pistol grips, it does not make the rear trigger less accessible. It is slightly more comfortable than a straight grip but does not seem to improve my shooting.

Gough Thomas's two qualities of balance, then, are helpful, but they do not settle the question. A riot gun could be well balanced by both of his measurements. Its sawed-off barrels and stock would certainly produce a low moment of inertia, and the balance-point might fall halfway between one's hands. Yet the gun would be useless for wing-shooting. We will have to look at two more qualities—not of the gun's middle, now, but of its extremities: stock-length and barrels.

3. *The stock.* When the shooting coach told me that I needed a full inch more length than I had been accustomed to using, I did not believe him. Still, I tried the new length because I had paid for advice and was too tight to waste money. A stock is easy to shorten, anyhow. I never had to do that: the coach was right. It seems that stock length is a function of both body and personality. I am long, scrawny, impetuous, and the only hunter you are likely to encounter carrying a sixteen-inch stock.

A long stock makes a gun slightly heavier to carry and slower to mount, but its main function is to push the whole weight farther from its pivot—my spine—after the gun is mounted. That gives it more inertia, making it slower to swing. A trick. Just what I needed.

4. *The barrels.* matter most of all because their weight is farthest from the gunner's body. The issue has been confused by discussions of the "sighting plane"—appearance, not weight. Mr. Robert Churchill, a good London gunmaker, claimed to have developed twenty-five-inch barrels that gave the impression of greater length because of a specially shaped rib. It was a selling point in the shop, meaningless in the field. When a gun is mounted, the sighting plane is so foreshortened that a difference of three inches is almost impossible to discern, even if you are looking for it. In the field, you should not be looking. You should see the barrels out of focus, a blur. Occasional gunmakers have lightened barrels by removing middle portions of the rib: not a bad idea.

Barrel Options

1. *Short barrels.* Instance my old Model 24 Winchester side-by-side double with twenty-six-inch barrels weighing exactly three pounds. Problem: though the gun's overall weight is heavy, it is still too fast to shoot, for me. I get the shot off quickly, but not accurately. A lighter, short-barreled gun might be right for you, but perhaps you should let a good coach watch you shooting before you bet on it.

2. *Long, heavy barrels.* Instance the same gun with its spare set of barrels, which are two inches longer and a full eight ounces heavier. Problem: Three-and-one-half-pound barrels would destroy the bal-

ance of any upland gun. This one is too heavy to carry and too muzzle-heavy to swing quickly. Such barrels might be right, however, for clay targets or ducks.

3. *Long, light barrels.* The 12-gauge Woodward's barrels are twenty-nine inches long and weigh two pounds fifteen ounces. The gun is light, easy to carry, fast to mount, and still precise. It offers not weight but inertia—a caution to me from out there at the barrels' tip. It encourages me to make the small, last-minute correction that is the difference between hitting and missing. For me, this seems to be the leading secret of the famous London balance.

I am not aware that anyone has discussed polar moment in detail, but Major Gerald Burrard explained its importance in this way: "If it were possible to concentrate all the weight of the gun between the hands, its inertia would be most easily overcome, but the gun could be moved round *too* easily and that degree of stability which is essential in shooting would be lost. For the inertia of *the forward part of the barrels* [my italics] helps one to steady the gun . . . and this is why some shooters find it difficult to shoot with very short-barrelled guns, while others find them a help."[4]

It would not be easy to measure polar moment, but here is an idea. Gene Hill writes that "virtually all 'good' guns have barrels that weigh . . . just about three pounds—regardless of whether they are twenty-six or thirty inches. Smaller gauges, twenties and twenty-eights, will of course weigh . . . less, but not much."[5] You might look for, say, a sixteen on a twenty-gauge frame, with long barrels. Then weigh those barrels before buying. Don't go over three pounds for the uplands. You will find, unfortunately, that light barrels cost more than heavy ones and are more fragile. Those on "best" guns are thick at the base for pressure, fairly thick at the muzzle for choking, and very thin in the middle for weight-saving.

Understand what all the fussing over a gun does. It helps at the margin. I have a friend who does not need help. He could have been a professional golfer but worked instead as floor boss for a gambling casino, overseeing characters who were fast of eye and hand. Sam's gun is a 20-gauge Browning autoloader with most of the choke reamed out. It is longer than my 12-gauge and probably weighs more. He cleans it once a year by spraying an all-purpose lubricant inside the action and barrel. When you see a fellow carrying a tool like that, with the bluing worn off, do not bet against him.

But there are those of us who need all the help we can get, plus a parable on hunting. Mr. Woodward supplied both. I do not know much about him. He was certainly a perfectionist. The gun was an altar for human sacrifice at a time when skilled workers earned pennies per hour. Every piece inside was finished with a compulsion transcending craftsmanship—even when the finish did not affect appearance or function.

Hunting matters if it is worth a gun built like a little cathedral. It chastens me when I shoot without respect, shirk the briars, take a shortcut back to the car. It is time then to pause for the hunter's equivalent of a tea ceremony. I whistle the dog in, sit, breathe, look to mountains beyond the stubble, run a finger over the gun's lines. Mr. Woodward was at pains to get them right.

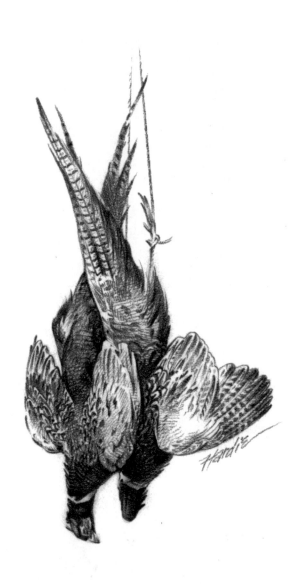

14

Flavor

. . . the essence of life is that it
lives by killing and eating; that's the
great mystery . . . You see, the basic
hunting myth is a kind of covenant
between the animal world and the human world.

Joseph Campbell[1]

This pheasant died for you. Bring him home for a dinner that you and your wife will cook, and thank him for his gift. It is the oldest marriage sacrament. You need it as much today as you needed it ten thousand years ago, though the pheasant's energy matters less now and his flavor more. What you have lost in desperation, you gain in smells and tastes, echoes that fill your house, myths recaptured.

Americans have a constitutional right to seek happiness, but in our ethos, its pursuit is dangerous. There is the risk of reaching for it and catching just pleasure. Happiness is a product of virtue and comes from chasing something of merit. Happiness is "a benefit we must pursue and conquer by the bold exercise of skill and energy . . . *La chasse au bonheur.*" It is the sum of "love + work,"[2] elusive in

137

the present, most accessible through memory. You catch happiness by recollecting emotion in tranquility.[3] You call it flavor.

Bringing out flavor is simple, the way Betty Bates did it. "Simple cooking isn't easy cooking,"[4] however, and I paid scant attention, back then: My part was the dragon-slaying. At least there was a flavor-memory, an assurance that game birds *could* taste good. Without that, it would have been easy to lose faith.

My wife and I, trying to recapture the flavor, worked our way through dishes varying from fair downwards. They came from books. Books are where book-people turn when they need help. We did not get it. On the most important parts, the "before side of the recipe" as John Thorne calls it,[5] I do not recall anything helpful. Information on aging and dressing was absent, evasive, or wrong. Authors who got into those subjects at all seemed to be reciting from old European texts with which they were not comfortable. Information on cooking methods—what works and what does not—was little better. Of the recipes themselves, most were recycled chicken dishes. A few food-writers today know what to do with a wild cock,[6] but the ones we found first perpetrated malpheasants.

- "Tough old cocks." The standard excuse for cooking them wrong. Properly aged and roasted, the long-spurred cocks have more flavor than the young ones and are almost as tender.
- Skinning. Removes the best-tasting part of the pheasant and the protective envelope that makes the roasting method possible.
- Clutter: fruits, brandy-flaming, olives, mushrooms, truffles, capers, and herb-mixtures. At best, the result is a sauce that you can eat with wild rice after you have pushed the bird to the back of your plate.
- Pen-raised pheasants. Better than chicken, but fatter and softer than wild birds and not flavored by berries, hips, seeds, nuts, and insects. Recipes based on tame birds may or may not work for wild ones. Most food-writers and restaurants deal with pen-raised pheasants. (American wild game may not legally be sold.)
- Open coals. If you grill over them, you cannot save the natural juices that drip off—a serious defect. (Roasting in the old way, with a drip-pan for the juices, ought to be ideal. But just try to find a spit and pan today.)

- High-fat methods. Pheasant tastes good larded, barded, or bubbled in fat. If the cock is small and has short, round spurs, try pan-frying him in bacon grease and making a gravy. But he tastes even better roasted with just two tablespoons of fat, and maybe low-fat cooking will keep you in the field a few years longer. (This is, to be sure, a terse epitaph for most of the pheasant recipes in the *Larousse Gastronomique*.)
- Moist-cooking methods. They give fair results for young pheasants cooked briefly: no longer than if they were roasted. But recipes often recommend prolonged stewing, braising, boiling, simmering, poaching, steaming, oven-bags, and clay-pot cooking for skinned birds and—yes—Tough Old Cocks. Don't believe it. The "pheasant over-boiled is poison."[7]

The problem is the chicken analogy. Pheasant is the anti-chicken. Chicken is young (about eight weeks for a broiler), force-grown by hormones, deprived of exercise and varied diet, flavorless. The pheasant is mature, natural, athletic, a hero in the field or on the Thanksgiving table. Chicken is fat, pheasant lean. Chicken needs no aging; pheasant needs much. Stewing makes old chickens tender, old pheasants stringy and dry. Chicken is bland and versatile, willing to absorb flavors. The pheasant fights back. You can cook flavor out of a pheasant but not into him. Make the most of what nature gave him.

Squeezing

They know how to make the most of things in Salto. It is a peasant village at the end of a gravel road in the Alentejo province of Portugal. It has no electricity, no plumbing, no television, no noise but people talking and sheep bleating. There is a spring where the women go for water and vineyards where the men work. There are a few rows of thick-walled houses that are whitewashed every month. Behind the houses are pigpens, pigeon coops, flocks of chickens running loose, and clay ovens that bake bread better than any you can buy in the whole of North America.

Henrique Granadeiro arrived in Salto on a Saturday in October with an unexpected American guest, so the women killed a pigeon to stretch the chicken dinner. It was served in two courses. The first, called *cabidela*, was rice in a brown sauce made from the blood of the birds. Floating around in the dish were the gizzards, hearts, livers, feet, and heads. The next dish was the rest of the birds. The revelation, for me, was that the *cabidela* was the best of the dishes. The flavors that we Americans throw away are better than the ones we keep. Perhaps it does not matter so much with pen-raised chickens: They are just meat. With pheasants you must think of capturing flavor instead of tissue. What you have, at the end, is "Above all other feathered game" (let alone chicken), but "few mortal men know how to present it at its best."[8]

Aging

Problems:

1. The modern assumption that meat should come fresh, fat, bland, scrubbed, and deprived of its mortality by a plastic wrap.

2. The pheasant's refusal, in cooking as in hunting, to fit even the older American ways. (No native bird that I have tried should be aged so long.[9])

3. Jean Anthelme Brillat-Savarin, 1755–1826.

The pheasant, he wrote, "when eaten within three days after its death, has nothing distinguishing about it. It is neither as delicate as a pullet, nor as savourous as a quail. At its peak of ripeness, however, its flesh is tender, highly flavored, and sublime".[10] So far, so good. Then Brillat-Savarin went on to say that the right moment is "when the pheasant begins to decompose". Generations of American food-writers have referred to this (directly or obliquely) and shuddered. Rotten meat, they have suggested, is all right for French perverts, but for us Yanks, no thanks.

Brillat-Savarin's terminology is too loose to be deciphered. All animals *begin* to decompose as soon as they die. The cells lose integrity as enzymes start to break down their structure. Some meats—including beef, venison, and pheasant—depend on this process for tenderness and flavor. You, dear sir or madam, eat partially decomposed beef in every good restaurant. If you think that you might like it fresh, try a trip to West Africa, where cattle are butchered and sold at the morning market. The best thing to be said for the product is that it provides good exercise for one's jaws.

Brillat-Savarin rules out pheasants eaten within three days. That might be enough aging if the birds were badly handled in the field

and then shipped to the market unrefrigerated, during warm weather.
In Europe, where wild game may be sold, some of it still reaches the
market over-ripe—and the pheasants usually taste good nevertheless.
There are abundant tales of people who seek out green-skinned
pheasants. During my years in European countries, however, I
did not meet either a green gourmet or a castle ghost. It was
disappointing.

From passing references to other birds in Brillat-Savarin's book,
I suspect that he liked pheasants aged at length. The recommendations hereafter, however, are not based on his book or any other.
They are based on the birds that my wife and I have dressed, aged,
and cooked. We learn new things every season, but what we recommend here will not get you in trouble. The pheasants will not seem
rotten. The contents of their body cavity will actually have a milder
smell after aging than when fresh. My young son complains about
almost all food except game birds, and of these he likes pheasants
best. So do not let Brillat-Savarin scare you off.

Field Treatment

The hunter is involved in this; he or she must cool and dry the bird
in the field. Get it out of the game-pocket as soon as possible. If the
weather is brisk—and it often is by the time pheasant season opens—
the best method is to hang the cock by *one* foot,[11] beak down, in a
dry, shady, breezy, insect-free, cool (but not freezing) place. The
inside of an old barn is perfect.

If the weather is warm, the process is a little different. Take
time soon after shooting the pheasant to pluck it around the vent,
then remove the intestine with your bird-knife's gut-hook or a forked
stick. Do not pluck the rest of the bird or open its body cavity yet.
Hang the pheasant long enough to dry it, if possible, and then put it
in an ice-chest till you get home. Arrange a shelf above the ice so
that the bird will not get wet.

Treatment at Home

Back home, if the bird is in good condition, hang it in full feather,
perfect. Its beauty will build your anticipation. It will reach its best
flavor, too: "Pheasants which are left in their feathers are much more

savory than those which have been naked for a long time," says Brillat-Savarin, and our experiments support that.

In Washington, I shot most pheasants on Saturdays. We plucked and dressed them eight days later, then cooked one for Sunday dinner. When there were two, we froze one for cooking later. A bird never became over-ripe in that time, and the flavor was almost always excellent. If you are new to the game, you might want to use eight days as a starting guideline—but keep an eye on the bird. Keep a nose on it, too. If you do, there will be no shocking surprises. Pheasants do not suddenly go bad all over like pears. If the bird starts to get too ripe, you will notice, usually in the skin surrounding the vent. Weather and the bird's condition are variables. Old cocks may well use a few extra days of aging. The process strikes us as fairly tolerant—not as fussy and mystical as you might guess from the literature. Perhaps this just means that we are not letting the aging go to the very last minute, as Brillat-Savarin may have done.

If the pheasant has been badly shot or chewed, hang it just long enough to cool and dry. Then pluck it and draw it. Age it in the refrigerator. Wire shelves allow better air circulation than glass. Plead with your spouse not to put the bird in a plastic bag until time for freezing.

Plucking is the only time-consuming part of the process. You have to do it a few feathers at a time, pulling with one hand and using the other to secure the skin, preventing tearing. Mechanical pluckers do not work. Scalding does, though it semi-cooks the skin.

If you are new to drawing birds, try to shake the notion that you are "cleaning" something. The only dirty pheasant you might find is the occasional pen-raised bird that has been released. Wild ones are fanatically clean.

Save and scrub the feet. Save and rinse the giblets. Rinse only the rear of the body cavity unless the bird has been badly shot. Pluck to the first joint of the wing. Skin and save the neck. Optionally, skin and save the head. It would be as easy to list what you throw out: intestines, crop, gizzard contents, and feathers. If you are a fly-tyer, you may want feathers too. Plucked, the bird will lose its beauty, but think of it as one of those old-fashioned, shriveled, tasty apples, as opposed to the shiny kind that tastes like styrofoam.

Pheasants are best if eaten as soon as the aging is completed, but the season does not last long enough to give you many dinners that way. A pheasant frozen in two bags will remain good for months, with none of the off-taste that you would expect from some frozen game. But do not look on freezing as a substitute for aging.

Mark the package with the bird's condition. If you shot it at close range, or if the dog left some pieces in such shape that they must be discarded, or if the skin is missing, you can at least save your honor. Cut the bird in small pieces and stir-fry, or make a soup. For the soup, remove the pheasant from its package and put it (still whole and frozen) into a stock pot with water. Simmer till tender. Remove and cut the meat into small pieces, returning them to the stock with diced vegetables: leeks, onions, garlic, carrots, celery, parsnip, and turnip, for example. If you happen to find these in the garden, so much the better; commercial carrots have become almost as tasteless as the tomatoes. Add herbs and seasonings to taste. Soup is the one dish that works for both chicken or pheasant, and probably for tyrannosaur. The difference between soup and most other moist-heat methods, I think, is that pieces of pheasant cut small can be eaten with a spoonful of broth for flavor.

If the bird is good, however, do not fool around. Roast it. Brillat-Savarin considered roast pheasant "worthy of being served to the angels themselves." A dish of them "was tasted with intense concentration; and all the time the ladies' eyes shone like stars, their lips gleamed like polished coral, and their faces were ecstatic." (His enthusiasms for angels, pheasants, and "the ladies" had much in common.)

Roast Pheasant with Dragon Sauce

1 cup bird stock (in an emergency, chicken broth)

1 bay leaf and six peppercorns

Pheasant aged & dressed as above, skin intact

1 tablespoon each butter and olive oil

Salt to taste

Wine to taste: sweet sherry, port, madeira, or marsala.

Twenty or thirty minutes before you start to roast the bird, heat the stock in a small saucepan. Add the bay leaf, peppercorns, feet, neck, skinned head, gizzard, heart, and any blood left from the body cavity or freezer bag. Simmer till the bird has finished roasting. Reserve the liver, uncooked.

Have the pheasant at room temperature for even roasting. Do not truss it or put the dressing in it; it would then cook less evenly and quickly, forcing you to overcook the breast meat in order to make the dressing safe. (My apologies to Brillat-Savarin. We have learned nothing about flavor since his day, but the study of medicine has progressed.)

Use a thick pan just a little larger than the pheasant, with raised sides. The best we have is a tin-lined, oval, copper pan ten inches long, of the kind used for small trout. In this, melt the butter and olive oil over medium heat till a drop of water sizzles when flicked in. Sear the bird on top of the range from as many angles as possible, turning with tongs and spatula. The breast skin and most of the rest should be brown.

Turn the bird on its back, add a splash of water to prevent the fat in the pan from burning, and put in an oven preheated to 350 degrees. Baste once with a brush after fifteen minutes, using the pan juices. After a total roasting time of thirty minutes (less if the bird is small), check. Lift the pheasant with tongs and pour the juices from its body cavity into the pan; they should be pink. Prick the breast with a sharp two-tined cooking fork; the juices that run out should be slightly pink or just clear. Occasional large birds may take another few minutes. (The thighs may need more cooking than the breast, but, as explained below, we normally reserve them for a second meal anyhow.)

At this point, things move fast. Enlist the help of spouse or guest. Put the bird on a carving board and cover with foil to keep warm. Pour the sweet wine into the roasting pan, scraping with the spatula to mix in anything stuck on the bottom. Pour in the simmering stock and all of its contents. Reduce at a slow boil while you *test for taste*, adding salt and more wine as needed. The tasting is essential. Once in awhile a pheasant fails to do his part and, if you have not used good stock, you must conduct a rescue operation with herbs, tabasco sauce, and an anchovy filet.

Pour contents of roasting pan through a strainer into a blender. Blend in the uncooked liver, sniffing first to be sure that it is good. It will cook instantly in the near-boiling pan juices. Pour what is now the sauce back into the small, empty pan in which the stock was simmered. Retrieve the heart and gizzard from the strainer; chop them and add to the sauce. Discard the rest of the material strained out of the stock, including coagulated blood. Reheat the sauce but do not boil, or the blood from the liver will coagulate.

The blood from the liver and body cavity will have made this a dragon sauce. It will have the same effect on you that dragon's blood did on Siegfried.

Carve the pheasant with a very sharp knife. Make a deep horizontal cut between wing and breast on each side, then slice the breast vertically into thin slices with a bit of skin (the best flavor of all) on each. Please do not spoil it all now by hacking off chunks with a dull knife. If you wish, serve the thighs and pick the good pieces off the back, but we reserve them with the legs and remainder of the meat for another dish to be described.

Plates should be warm. Spoon sauce over the sliced meat, dressing, and the best green vegetable you have (such as kale or asparagus, but not zucchini). Think of the dressing not as a separate dish but as a pheasant-surrogate that soaks up sauce and rewards you with concentrated flavor. If the whole bird were now stolen by Brillat-Savarin's angels, you could still have an excellent pheasant dinner with just dressing and sauce. This is why we can serve two adults and a child on the breast of one pheasant.

Ask everyone to eat as soon as served. No waiting for the hostess.

Caution: do not rehearse this dish with chicken. The sauce will fail.

Dressing

1 cup shallots, chopped

1 cup celery, diced

2 tablespoons butter

6 ounces dried bread crumbs, by weight

½ to ¾ cup milk (or fresh cream)

2 cups chestnuts, shelled and partially cooked

Small bunch fresh parsley, chopped

Salt & pepper to taste

Soften the shallots and celery in the melted butter, with a lid on the pan to preserve the liquid. Pour over the bread crumbs and mix well. Add enough milk to moisten. Add the chestnuts and mix again.

Heat as much dressing as you need in the top of a double-boiler, starting before the pheasant goes in the oven. Freeze the rest (probably about half of the above).

Fresh cream improves the dressing, though we usually omit it. Use another herb instead of the parsley if you prefer, but do not exaggerate.

Chestnuts are important but difficult to get fresh. Get dried ones, if you can find a source, and soften by boiling in a little water till soft but not disintegrating. Add both nuts and water to the dressing. Or get canned chestnuts at vast expense. Break each nut in half to check for worms. In a pinch, substitute pecans. There is nothing original in this dressing, but we have worked out what seems to taste best.

Wines

The sweet wine used in the sauce should be of decent quality, but not expensive. No wine retains subtle flavors when boiled. Sherries, real or spurious, are often good enough at a modest price. Port runs to extremes, and the best of it is too good for anything except sipping with dessert.

Brillat-Savarin settled the matter of table wines for a century. "This highly savorous dish should be accompanied, preferably, by a vintage Burgundy; I have reached this conclusion after a series of observations which have been more work to me than a table of logarithms." Problem: There are more pheasants around than bottles of vintage Burgundy, and the people who can catch the former are generally not those who can afford the latter. Great bottles of Bordeaux are almost as far out of reach. Writers who keep on recommending this stuff are not helping much. There are three possibilities: They get it free, spend a lot of money on it, or do not drink enough of it to be credible. So let us start over.

The wine should be as well-aged as the pheasant. Avoid raw, young wines that you might like with acid sauces. Serve anything else you enjoy, including chilled white or "blush" (rose) if your stock of birds lasts till a hot summer evening. Suppose, however, that you are hoarding a big, old red wine—one so good that you decide to reverse the normal order of things and choose the dinner to suit the wine. In that case, choose roast pheasant and one close friend of the opposite sex. Then skip the recorded music; Brillat-Savarin's angels are going to sing the Alleluia Chorus for you.

Of the good red varietals, all that we have tried seem capable of producing the right wine. None are too full-bodied to go well with pheasants. (It is another case where the chicken analogy must be avoided.) Mostly we get wines of the Petite Sirah and Cabernet Sauvignon grapes, which are easily available. Some Zinfandels work, and one of the best was a dry Portuguese table wine made of the same grapes used for sweet Port. For now, look among reds from Australia, California, Portugal, Spain, and Chile; but that will change. Buy for flavor (which you can drink) rather than price, label, or prestige (which you cannot). Find a wine merchant who can do better than suggesting that you get what you pay for, because you don't.

The Second Meal

While one of you is washing the dishes, the other cuts the leftovers away from bone and tendon. There should be two full cups if you include thighs, legs, wings, skin, and all the delicious little scraps on the carcass.

We make a second meal out of the pheasant because he is, for cooking, two birds. The white-meated breast is the grand prize, easily ruined by overcooking or moist heat. The rest of the bird—mostly dark meat—remains good after simmering. At last you can make complicated things. Try a pie with pheasant pieces, walnuts, and the remaining sauce (which helps greatly). This will do justice to any wine left in your bottle.

For a low-fat method, try a stir-fry with the same vegetables recommended for soup, except that you slice (julienne) instead of dicing. Add the pheasant pieces, and leftover sauce. Use sherry, salt and fresh black pepper to taste. Serve over green pasta shells.

The Third Meal

If you tried the stir-fry, turn any that you do not finish at the first sitting into a polenta made with the best cornmeal you can find. Eat a green salad while it is cooking. With the polenta itself—well, it is time to open another bottle of wine. I suppose that this dish can finally be considered leftovers, but you will not feel deprived. It does not take very much essence of pheasant to furnish a lot of flavor.

Stock

You did not, surely, expect that I would let you throw away the carcass. Freeze the bones and scraps of all game birds till you have enough to fill a stock pot. Simmer all day with celery stalks and leaves, carrots, and onions. The stock should simmer down until, when chilled, it will form a gelatin. Strain and pour in one-cup amounts into the bottom of small containers. Freeze, remove from containers, put each bit of frozen stock in a plastic bag, and thaw one when you have the next pheasant to cook.

That will do it. Remember that a cook, like a businessman, makes his profit at the margins, by squeezing out every last bit of efficiency, or flavor. It is the small difference between a business that is profitable or bankrupt, a pheasant that is first-class or pushed around the plate.

I forgot to tell you to save the wishbone and break it at the next pheasant dinner with appropriate wishes, then throw the broken bits in with the bones for the stock. May this bring you luck and pheasants. They are the same thing.

Notes

Chapter 1

[1] Kristofferson, Kris. "Me & Bobby McGee," in Janice Joplin's *Pearl* album. NY: Columbia Records, undated.

[2] Usage note: *Phasianus colchicus* is the only bird implied when I use the term "pheasant." In this country, its gene pool may include a mixture of several races (some thirty-one of which are spread across vast areas of Asia). Our common pheasant usually looks like the Chinese ring-necked race, *P.c. torquatus*. It behaves in the same way and lives in the same kinds of cover wherever I have hunted in America and Europe. Other races, however, are still being introduced. My most recent source for this and much other information is: Hallett, D.L., W.R. Edwards, and G.V. Burger (eds.). *Pheasants: Symptoms of Wildlife Problems on Agricultural Lands.* Bloomington, IN: North Central Section of the Wildlife Society, 1988.

[3] Our most abundant game bird is probably the dove. It is migratory and about one-tenth the weight of the pheasant, so that greater numbers can survive the scarcities of winter. Of the gallinaceous birds, only the bobwhite seems to be more abundant than the pheasant. About 35 million bobwhites were shot in 1970, as opposed to half that many pheasants (some 16 or 18 million) in their peak years. I am surprised that the difference is not greater. The bobwhite is about one-seventh the pheasant's weight, occupies a range of roughly similar area, and lives where there is more food and cover in the winter. The source of the above statistics is: Terres, John K. *The Audubon Society Encyclopedia of North American Birds.* NY: Knopf, 1982.

Chapter 2

[1] I think that I am borrowing struggle and chance—*agon* and *alea*—from Roger Callois, via Raymond Aron. I have not run my source to ground, however. Writing is easy in Montana; research has its problems.

[2] Campbell, Joseph. *The Power of Myth*. NY: Doubleday, 1988, pp. 149/150. He gave me the eagle's beak and serpent's tail; confirmed that my dragon was the real thing. You might be interested in knowing, however, that I had my dragon (and this book) in draft before reading Campbell. Discovering the universality of dragons was a shivery feeling.

[3] Many of the thoughts in this sentence come from Herbert Mitgang's review in the *New York Times* (April 14, 1989) of a book by James McGregor Burns (*The Crosswinds of Freedom*: NY: Knopf, 1989).

[4] Bloom, Allan. *The Closing of the American Mind*. NY: Simon & Schuster, 1987. p. 134.

[5] "From Blue Duns to Woolly Buggers," *Trout* magazine, Summer 1989, p. 78.

Chapter 3

[1] Stuart-Wortley, A.J. *The Pheasant*. Southampton: Ashford Press, 1986 (first edition 1895), pp. 5, 70. The quotation is from Gervase Markham's "tiny duodecimo volume, entitled 'Hunger's Prevention; or, The Whole Art of Fowling by Water and Land,' published in London in 1655."

[2] "Pheasant" is as close as English speakers can come to pronouncing the Greek *Phasianos*, "the Phasian (bird)," from the River Phasis. The river is no longer called that, so the bird's name has outlasted even that of its homeland.

[3] Hen pheasants do, however, have the bad habit of laying eggs in any nest they come across (and sometimes in no nest at all). This "nest parasitism" may be at the expense of native prairie grouse.

[4] Weigand, John P. and Reuel G. Janson. *Montana's Ring-Necked Pheasant*. Montana Department of Fish and Game, 1976, p. 2. For more on the history, see: Allen, Durward L., ed. *Pheasants in North America*. Harrisburg: Stackpole, 1956.

[5] Betten, H.L. *Upland Game Shooting*. Philadelphia: Penn, 1940. pp. 18–22.

[6] Wright, Leonard M., Jr., ed. *The Field & Stream Treasury of Trout Fishing*. NY: Winchester/Lyons, 1986, p. 12.

[7] This is a British opinion. Stuart-Wortley, A.J. *The Pheasant*. Southampton: Ashford Press, 1986 (first edition 1895), p. 149.

[8] There are two or three good books on pheasants, the most recent being: Steve Grooms. *Modern Pheasant Hunting*. Harrisburg: Stackpole, 1987. At this writing, I am not aware of any books where the pheasant and pointer meet with much frequency. Some references to pheasants and pointers (like Betten's) are identified in footnotes. All of these are from books, but there have been good magazine articles too. I have made no systematic attempt to search periodicals.

[9] I want to express my appreciation to the members of this club, and especially to those who helped me work through the material on dogs:

Tom Eversman, Dennis Kavanagh, Jeff Koski, Butch Nelson, and Larry Michnevich.

[10] "Upland game birds," these days, are almost all that live mainly on land rather than water. All gallinaceous birds are considered upland game because they are hunted in similar ways—by people and dogs walking rather than boating or waiting in a blind, as for waterfowl. But this is a hunter's definition, not the dictionary's, and it has changed over the years. It does not accurately describe the pheasant, which likes to be near water and gets along well in marshes. Think of the pheasant as a bird of mixed country: fields, patches of brush or trees, gentle hills, wet spots, and grain if available.

Chapter 5

[1] Hammond, S.T. *My Friend the Partridge*. Auburn, MI: The Gunnerman's Press, undated (first edition 1898), p. 7.

[2] Foster, William Harnden. *New England Grouse Shooting*. NY: Scribner's, 1942.

[3] The nouns "cover" and "covert" have the same origin and are so close that we hardly need both—but that's the English language for you. I have tried to use "covert" to describe the place where game lives and "cover" to describe its vegetation.

[4] The first edition of Spiller's *Grouse Feathers* was published in 1935.

[5] I offer this footnote not for the 1990s but for anyone who finds himself confused in, say, another five-hundred years. In 1989, National Public Radio broadcast an interview with a photographer who criticized a painter's representational work as "banal." The photographer-critic was, in his words, "into body fluids."

[6] "Edward Panofsky, Dürer's definitive biographer, remarks that 'every hair on the fur of the little hare and every grass and herb in a piece of turf are studied and rendered with a devotion closely akin to religious worship.'" In *Natural History* magazine, September 1989, p. 80.

[7] pp. 39–42.

[8] Anonymous. *The Sportsman's Companion*. NY: Robertsons, Mills, & Hicks, 1783. My edition is the Stackpole reprint of 1948. The author was apparently a British officer stationed in New York City. When he mentions "grouse" nearby, he is referring only to the heath hen—a now-extinct relative of the prairie chicken. He also mentions hunting for bobwhite quail on "New York Island." There must have been ruffed grouse around, but perhaps they were considered, in Hammond's words (footnote 1), "unsatisfactory . . . to pursue for sport."

Chapter 6

[1] Macpherson, H.A. *The Pheasant*. Southampton: Ashford Press, 1986, p. 46–49.

Chapter 7

[1] Leopold, Aldo. Cited in *Smithsonian* magazine, November 1989, p. 44. Attributed to "his 1933 handbook on game management."
[2] Hallett, D.L. et al. *Pheasants: Symptoms of Wildlife Problems on Agricultural Lands*. Bloomington, IN: North Central Section of The Wildlife Society, 1988, pp. 29–43.
[3] Allen, Durward L. *Pheasants in North America*. Harrisburg: Stackpole, 1956, p. 52.
[4] *Pheasants Forever* magazine, Winter 1990, p. 14–16.
[5] Hallett, p. 161.
[6] The *New York Times* September 8, 1989, p. 1.
[7] Leopold, Aldo. *A Sand County Almanac*. NY: Oxford University Press, 1949.
[8] Hallett, p. 181.
[9] Hallett, p. 18.
[10] Hallett, p. 11.
[11] Ortega y Gasset, Jose. *Meditations on Hunting*. NY: Scribner's, 1985, p. 97.
[12] Hallett, pp. 12, 207.
[13] Hallett, p. 7.
[14] Macpherson, H.A. *The Pheasant*. Southampton: Ashford Press, 1986 (first edition 1895), pp. 173, 178.

Chapter 9

[1] Allen, Durward L. *Pheasants in North America*. Harrisburg: Stackpole, 1956, p. 27.
[2] Ortega y Gasset, Jose. *Meditations on Hunting*. NY: Scribner's, 1985, p. 76.
[3] One old recommendation for a pheasant dog: Hawker, Lt. Col. P. *Instructions For Young Sportsmen In All That Relates To Guns And Shooting*. London: Longman, 1830, p. 156.

Chapter 10

[1] Foster, William Harnden. *New England Grouse Shooting*. NY: Scribner's, 1942, Chapter II.
[2] Foster, William H(arnden). *Bird Dogs in New England*. Oelgart, 1984. Unpaginated. (Reproduction of a paper read in 1930.)

[3] Bravo, João Maria. *O Ensino do Cão da Caça*. Lisbon: Diana, 1986.

[4] Fly fishermen will recognize the homage to Vincent Marinaro's *A Modern Dry-Fly Code*, first published in 1950.

[5] From Yeats, W.B. "Among School Children." In *The Tower*, 1928.

Chapter 11

[1] Bernstein, Jeremy. "A Critic At Large (The Einstein-Besso Letters)." *New Yorker* magazine, February 27, 1989, p. 92.

[2] Arkwright, William. *The Pointer And His Predecessors*. London: Humphreys, 1902. My thanks to Judith Bowman for providing the illustration from Arkwright.

[3] Bravo, João Maria. *O Ensino do Cão da Caça*. Lisbon: Diana, 1986. This is, oddly, the only recent work I know of that explores the origins of the pointing dog. It drew my attention to Pisanello's model, of which João Bravo shares Arkwright's high opinion. He makes a case that the English pointer may have derived from a Portuguese original, and in fact the English dog much more closely resembles the Portuguese than the "Spanish pointer" to which the English gave credit. The term "Spanish pointer" seems to have been used at one time for any Iberian pointing dog.

[4] This description draws from an Italian engraving dated 1622, appearing in Arkwright and Bravo. It shows dogs that are modern both in appearance and pointing style.

[5] Foster, William H(arnden). *Bird Dogs in New England*. Oelgart, 1984. Unpaginated. (Reproduction of a paper read in 1930.)

[6] Anonymous. *The Sportsman's Companion*. Harrisburg: Stackpole, 1948 (reprint of a book that first appeared in 1783), p. 8.

[7] For this description of a functional body, I have drawn heavily on "The Beauty Contest," a column by Bill Tarrant in *Field & Stream*, August, 1987, pp. 102–104.

[8] You should take this as my prejudiced version of the history, because it is certainly too brief to be balanced. I condensed it from Jim McCue's "This is the Shorthair" in *Gun Dog* magazine, March/April 1989, p. 37.

[9] Dave Duffey in *Gun Dog* magazine, October/November, 1989, p. 23.

Chapter 13

[1] A start would be Bob Brister's book, identified below, and Stephen Bodio's *Good Guns* (NY: Nick Lyons Books, 1986). There has also been a blossoming of magazines on the subject: *Shooting Sportsman*, *Gun Dog* (Don Zutz), and *Double Gun Journal*.

[2] Thomas, Gough (G.T. Garwood). *Shotguns & Cartridges for Game and Clays*. London: A & C Black, 1981, pp. 158–164.

[3] Brister, Bob. *Shotgunning*. NY: Winchester, 1977, p. 102.

[4] Burrard, Major Sir Gerald. *The Modern Shotgun* Volume I (The Gun). London: Herbert Jenkins, 1951, p. 133-4.

[5] Hill, Gene. *Gun Dog* magazine, May/June 1989, p. 57.

Chapter 14

[1] Campbell, Joseph. *The Power of Myth.* NY: Doubleday, 1988, pp. xvi, 72.

[2] The quotations in the paragraph to this point are from Michiko Kakutani's review in the *New York Times* of December 31, 1988 (p. 13). The book reviewed is Peter Quennell's *The Pursuit of Happiness* (NY: Little, Brown & Company). The authorities cited are Samuel Johnson, Turgenev, Byron, Proust, Aristotle, John Stuart Mill, George Washington, Balzac, and Stendahl. I am seldom in such good company.

[3] "poetry . . . takes its origin from emotion recollected in tranquillity." William Wordsworth, from his preface to the *Lyrical Ballads.*

[4] Thorne, John. *Simple Cooking.* NY: Penguin, 1989, p. xxi.

[5] p. xxvii.

[6] Sylvia Bashline describes uncluttered cooking in a monthly column for *Field & Stream.* I should confess, however, that we seldom cook by recipe these days, which means that I have not done a thorough search and must beg the pardon of good pheasant cooks who have not been mentioned.

[7] Macpherson, H.A. *The Pheasant.* Southampton: Ashford Press, 1986 (first edition 1895), p. 259.

[8] Brillat-Savarin, Jean Anthelme. *The Physiology of Taste.* NY: Knopf, 1971 (first edition 1826), p. 87. This is the excellent translation by M.F.K. Fisher, whose notes improve the book. Brillat-Savarin spent some years in America and must have eaten our ruffed grouse, but he does not mention it. In my view, the ruffed (and blue) grouse are less consistent than pheasants but can be as good.

[9] With sage grouse and sharptailed grouse, it is safest to pluck and draw right away, aging in the refrigerator until eaten. We hang ruffed grouse and bobwhites like pheasants, but they reach peak flavor quickly. Leigh Perkins experimented and found four days good. This is from personal conversation and the Orvis Cookbook, which has a good chapter on method and aging. (Perkins, Romi. *Game in Season.* NY: Nick Lyons Books, 1986.)

[10] Brillat-Savarin, p. 374. Remaining quotations in this chapter are from pp. 374-376.

[11] In a bird hung head-down, the feathers fall open, exposing the skin to air circulation. The entrails also fall away from the vent, avoiding spoilage in that sensitive area. This is explored in: Holland, Ray P. *Scattergunning.* NY: Knopf, 1951, Chapter XXII. My contribution is hanging by a single leg, which best ventilates the ventral area. Many old paintings show birds hung that way, so the practice is not original.